To Abdel
great friend [illegible]
a long long time.
With friendship
and affection.

Vito Tanzi
Oct 2, 2014

Russian Bears and Somali Sharks

Russian Bears and Somali Sharks

Transition and Other Passages

by

Vito Tanzi

Jorge Pinto Books Inc.
New York

JORGE
PINTO
BOOKS

Russian Bears and Somali Sharks: Transition and Other Passages

Published by Jorge Pinto Books Inc., website: www.pintobooks.com

Book design by Charles King, website: www.ckmm.com

ISBN10: 1-934978-36-1
ISBN13: 978-1-934978-36-8

Contents

Preface • *xi*

Part One: Transition from Communism:
Russia, Hungary, Croatia • 1

Chapter 1:
Russia Around 1990 • 3
Chapter 2:
The Bolshevik Experiment • 19
Chapter 3:
Russia: When the IMF Danced with the Bear • 31
Chapter 4:
Russia in the Late 1990s • 46
Chapter 5:
Putin's Russia • 57
Chapter 6:
Hungary: From Central Plan to the European Union • 69
Chapter 7:
Croatia: From Central Planning and War to Peace • 93

Part Two: Other Passages:
Portugal, Somalia, Lebanon, Morocco • 107

Chapter 8:
Portugal: Transition from Salazar • 109
Chapter 9:
Portugal: Rejoining Europe • 120
Chapter 10:
Somalia: The Slaughterhouse and the Sharks • 139
Chapter 11:
Lebanon: Transition from Civil War • 153
Chapter 12:
Morocco: Transition from Colonialism and from Overregulation • 165

Dedication

To the Young Ones

Nicolas, Stephanie, Emilio, Lorenzo

and

Bellamina and Mia

Preface

Like people, countries occasionally experience intense and radical changes that take them from one stage to different stages. For people, the changes are caused by marriages, divorces, losses of dear ones, retirements, loss of jobs, major illnesses or accidents, and so on. For countries the changes are caused by transitions from one economic or political system to others; or from war to peace; or, occasionally, the other way around. Advanced countries, with well-established political or economic systems, are less likely to experience these intense changes than other countries.

This book covers seven countries that, in recent decades, underwent what could be considered significant transformations. Three of them—Russia, Hungary, and Croatia—moved from central planning, and from the domination of communist parties, to market economies, with more democratic regimes. Part I of this book deals with these countries. A large part of it, the first five chapters, covers Russia. The second part of the book—Part II—deals with four countries that experienced other kinds of transitions. They are Portugal, Somalia, Lebanon and Morocco.

For all seven countries, the description is based on trips that I took over four decades and on works that I did in them, mainly as an employee of the International Monetary Fund. Many anecdotes provide some entertainment and convey direct information on developments in these countries. The book is obviously not a technical book written for experts and should not be judged from that perspective; rather, it has been written for general readers who have some interest in transitions and in the countries covered. Hopefully, experts may also find some useful information in it, especially in the section on Russia. The main objective of the book is to inform while at the same time to entertain the readers. It is a book to be read during a long plane ride or during a vacation. Because the descriptions are based on direct, personal, experiences and observations, and not on library research, there is a freshness to them that is often lacking in more technical books. This freshness may have come at the price of some factual errors.

This is the fourth and last of a series of four books that, to some limited extent, can be considered as an impressionistic tour of the world. The other three were: *Argentina: An Economic Chronicle*

(2007); *Peoples, Places, and Policies: China, Japan and Southeast Asia* (2008); and *The Charm of Latin America* (2010). They represent a kind of extensive debriefing on almost five decades of professional involvement in many countries of the World. Eighteen countries are covered in these four books.

I would like to thank few people for the help that they provided me on this book. Professor Hilary Appel, of Claremonth McKenna College, and Anna and Anders Åslund gave me some useful comments on the chapters on Russia. Of course, they are not responsible in any way for the views expressed and for any errors in the descriptions. Many more people could be thanked for having provided indirect help during the many years covered by the book. Some of their names are in the various chapters. Francesca Caparas competently edited the manuscript, and Jesusa Hilario, patiently typed several drafts of it. I would also like to thank my wife, Maria, for her patience in feeding and taking care of the zombie like creature who roamed the house and spent much of his time at his desk, working and writing, while showing no interest whatsoever in any other activities.

—Vito Tanzi
August 6, 2010
Bethesda, Md.

Part One

Transition from Communism

Russia

Hungary

Croatia

Chapter I

Russia Around 1990

Until 1991, I had not been to Russia or, for that matter to any part of the Soviet Union. The little I knew about that part of the world came mostly from newspaper articles. In 1959, just after completing my BA in economics, I worked for six months for a congressional study group headed by a young professor at Harvard, Otto Eckstein. Senator Paul Douglas, then head of the Joint Economic Committee (JEC) in the U.S. Congress, had hired him to conduct a congressional study of the economic growth and inflation in the United States. I had been hired as a research assistant for the group of prominent economists that Professor Eckstein had assembled in Washington to conduct the study.

A major concern, and one reason for the study, was that the Soviet Union, at that time, was growing at a much higher rate than the United States. Perhaps even more worrisome was the fact that the Soviet Union's steel production was forecast to soon exceed that of the USA. Steel production was then considered a major index of military power. It was what countries needed to make tanks and cannons. In this period the Russians had put Sputnik into space, an event that had sent shock waves through the U.S. political and military establishment. CIA estimates of the economic and military potential of the Soviet Union had generated much more anxiety than that generated in 2001 by the news of Iraqi weapons of mass destruction. At the end of 1959, the study group published the "Eckstein's Report," a report that Ted Sorensen, in his biographical book of the Kennedy years, credited as having had a major impact on President Kennedy's thinking. Kennedy had exploited the CIA's estimates of a presumed "missile gap" in his presidential campaign against Nixon, just as Bush exploited the news about the weapons of mass destruction to justify the Iraq War.

Despite the work I had done for Professor Eckstein in 1959, which had introduced me at least superficially to the system of central planning in Russia, it was not until August 1991 that I had my first direct involvement with Russia. While working for the IMF, where I was then the Director of the Fiscal Affairs Department, I was also President of the International Institute of Public Finance (IIPF).

The IIPF is a largely academic, international institution, established in France in the 1930s, with its routine work done by a secretariat in a German university (now the University of Munich). The IIPF membership is made up of public finance scholars, mostly university professors, from many different countries. At that time the membership included also scholars from the Soviet Union and from several Eastern European countries.

As President of the IIPF, I had to arrange the Institute's annual congresses. These congresses take place each year in late August in countries selected several years beforehand by the IIPF Board. In these countries, local sponsors have agreed to cover the local costs of the congresses and to make the local arrangements for them. During normal years, the President's work is limited to a few days a year and involves some basic decisions, such as determining the theme of the Congress, the choice of the scientific committee and its chairman, and so on. However, 1991 did not turn out to be a normal year. As was the praxis, the location for the 1991 Congress had been selected a few years earlier, when the Soviet Union seemed to be a very stable area. The participants from Russia had invited the IIPF to hold the 1991 Congress in Leningrad (now St. Petersburg), and the IIPF Board had accepted this invitation. At the time of the decision, when Mikhail Gorbachev was the general secretary of the Central Committee of the Communist Party of the Soviet Union, no one could have anticipated the dramatic changes that would occur in the Soviet Union during those years. In March 15, 1990 Gorbachev was elected president of the USSR by the USSR Congress of People's Deputies. On May 29, 1990 Boris Yeltsin was elected chairman of the new Russian Congress of People's Deputies. On June 12, 1990 Russia was declared a sovereign state and on June 12, 1991 Yeltsin became the first, popularly elected president of Russia. In August 1991, the Russian Communist party was disbanded, and by December 1991 the Soviet Union no longer existed and broke down into many new, independent countries.

As the date of the Congress approached, the Russian members of the IIPF insisted that all was in order on their side and that the Leningrad Congress should be held as planned, in spite of the ongoing economic and political chaos. They reported that they had managed to organize the space and to get the financial resources for the social functions (banquets, dinners, sightseeing tours, etc.) required by the Congress.

The week before the IIPF Congress was to start I had made

arrangements for my wife and myself to leave Washington for Leningrad. On the Monday of that week, rumors began circulating about an impending coup against Gorbachev in Russia. By Tuesday the coup was in full swing. The four-hundred participants, coming from some sixty countries around the world, would soon be leaving their places of residence to go to Leningrad as the Congress was set to begin the following weekend. Many would be accompanied by their spouses and some even by their children. I started receiving phone calls and cables from many IIPF members telling me that they had cancelled their trip, and from others asking me what they should do. Should they leave for Leningrad? Was the Congress still on? As the hours passed, the situation in Moscow and in Leningrad sounded progressively more ominous. On Tuesday, *The Financial Times* had a front-page picture of tanks moving towards the Russian White House in Moscow. *The New York Times* reported that hundreds of thousands of people were demonstrating in the streets and in the squares of Leningrad and Moscow. I was hesitant to make a decision. In that period my blood pressure must have sky-rocketed, and I must have been subjected to one of the highest levels of stress in my life.

On Tuesday I finally decided that it would be irresponsible of me to send hundreds of people to Leningrad under circumstances that could have easily deteriorated into street fighting or civil war. Thus, given the information that I had available at that time, I made the only decision that to me seemed rational: I decided to cancel the meeting. However, there was the logistical problem of informing the participants, who were scattered around the world, at a time when internet communication was not yet available. With the help of my highly efficient assistant at the IMF, Mrs. Pamela Palco, I informed as many registered participants as I could reach by phone that the meeting was cancelled. Fortunately, I also received many calls from prospective participants who were still undecided. This facilitated my efforts to spread the information.

With hindsight my decision turned out to be disastrously wrong. By Thursday the coup had collapsed and it became obvious that the meeting could have taken place as planned. Given how difficult it must have been on the Russian side to prepare for this meeting under such circumstances, the Russian organizers were rightly very upset with my decision to cancel the meeting. After the coup I received some calls from prospective participants, including some who had decided on their own initiative not to go, complaining about my decision. I also learned later that a few IIPF members, from countries such as Argentina and China, had left early, unaware of what was going on in Russia, had gone to Leningrad, and had even enjoyed their visit.

Over the years I have often wondered whether I should have made a different decision. However, I have generally concluded, perhaps in my own self interest, that with the knowledge I had had at the time, it was the only responsible and rational decision that I could have made. The problem was that, once the decision had been made, it became impossible to reverse it within the necessary time and given the technology of the time. To contact the IIPF members would have required a lot of time and by then many would have already cancelled their flights.

This decision not only had a substantial psychological and, perhaps, reputational cost for me, but also a financial cost of about two-thousand dollars. I had bought plane tickets for my wife and myself, on a Pan American Airlines flight. When we did not use the tickets, Pan Am gave us vouchers for future flights. Unfortunately, before we could use the vouchers, Pan Am went bankrupt and quickly disappeared. Perhaps losing this money was some kind of retribution. I took a tax deduction for this monetary loss, so that indirectly the U.S. government shared in the loss.

Coincidentally, I went to Moscow on behalf of the IMF three months later, in December 1991, to participate in initial discussions regarding Russia's application to become a member of the Fund. By that time the Soviet Union had collapsed and a Russian reform Government headed by a young economist, Yegor Gaidar, had been formed in November. Gorbachev would resign as president of the no-longer existing USSR on December 25, 1991. Several Fund employees were already in Moscow at the invitation of the Russian authorities, some from my own departments. They were there to begin a process of technical assistance to Russia in various areas that lasted for a decade during which the Russian economy made a transition from central planning toward a yet-evolving market economy.

When I arrived in Moscow, my colleague Isaias Coelho, a Brazilian who worked in my department, met me at the airport. I had made reservations at the famous Hotel Metropol, a historical hotel that was reported to be the best hotel in Moscow at that time. The Metropol is located a short walk from the Kremlin and occupies a beautiful building. The hotel had a magnificent breakfast room where, I recall, in the morning, a blond girl with an angelic look played a harp while the guests enjoyed their breakfast. However, despite the luxurious surrounding, the hotel rooms did not have telephones in working order. This created a serious personal problem because my (first) wife at that time had started having major health problems as a consequence of her breast cancer. After nine years in remission, the cancer had returned. She would lose her fight against it four years later. During this visit to Russia, I had great difficulties in contacting her.

This was also the period when food scarcity hit Russia, and dining in Moscow became a big problem. Food scarcity had become a major topic of discussion and a constant preoccupation for those traveling to Moscow. Newspaper articles were predicting mass starvation in Russia. At that time, IMF staff was visiting Moscow in increasing numbers. They would often leave Washington with suitcases full of dry food in the event that food became unavailable for several days.

The day after my arrival to Moscow, I visited the Supreme Soviet and the Tax Administration accompanied by some colleagues from my department. The goal was to establish contacts with relevant individuals and offices and to familiarize ourselves with the existing Russian system of taxation and budgeting. At the time none of us had much knowledge of how the Russian public finances operated. How did the government get its tax revenue? What taxes did it use? How did it prepare its budget? How inclusive was the budget? What were the relations between the center government and the regions? How did the tax administration operate? Did Russia have a treasury office? These were some of the questions to which we did not have precise answers and which were of concern to the IMF. We needed these answers in order to organize the technical assistance that the IMF would provide to Russia and to be able to design financial programs in future years that would make IMF loans available to Russia.

These first visits were useful for establishing contacts with some of the individuals with whom we would interact over the following years. However, they also highlighted a recurring problem, one which would occasionally prove to be serious: that of the meaning and application of terms. We had run into a similar problem in China a few years earlier when China became a Fund member. During our many long discussions with officials, we would rely on interpreters without realizing that the same terms had different meanings for us and for them. For example, at our first meeting with Russian policymakers at the Supreme Soviet, we were told that the government intended to reform the income tax. There was a long description of this reform that left us totally perplexed and confused. Only later did we realize that for the Russians "income" meant the *total revenue* that enterprises received from sales, rather than the profits or other forms of what we call income—that is, the difference between total revenue and allowed costs. In Russia there was no concept of "income" as that concept is understood in market economies. Thus, all the time the Russian counterparts were talking about the reform of the sales taxes while we were thinking about the reform of the income tax. This experience showed me the merit of Ludwig Joseph Wittengstein's views on language. He argues that languages reflect common experiences shared by those who speak a given language. In other words, for translators to be able to translate in a meaningful way, the two sides must have shared common experiences. Two people with different experiences and different languages cannot mechanically translate one language into the other because some of the experiences reflected in the words of one party will not have been shared by the other. This linguistic problem—a kind of asymmetry in information—is much more common than is realized.

Other terms which created misunderstanding were "equilibrium price" and "ruble zone." For us, equilibrium price meant the price at which demand and supply meet so that buyers can buy and sellers can sell what they want at that price. However, in an economy in which people had money to spend but shops had little or nothing to sell, and what they sold had prices fixed administratively, there was no equilibrium price. When goods arrived in a shop, prospective buyers would wait in long lines and empty the shelves in little time. In these circumstances, the prices did not play the function of adjusting demand to supply and vice versa, as they normally do in market economies. For many consumers, goods buying stopped when the shelves in the shops became empty. Thus, the availability of goods, assumed by an equilibrium price, was either interpreted as a case of "saturation" of the market, that is, of the production of unwanted goods; or, more frequently, it was assumed that people were too poor to buy the available goods. In later years a common refrain became: "before we had money but there were no goods to buy; now that there are goods we have no money." Thus, the view was that the scarcity of goods had been followed by the scarcity of money. This was partly the result of the liberalization of prices in January 1992 that wiped out the value of the financial assets that Russians had and sharply reduced real wages.

When the first visitors from the transition economies started coming to Washington, often to attend training courses at the teaching institute of the Fund (the IMF Institute), or to discuss economic policies, they would be taken to visit the shopping malls. At first they were amazed by the quantity of goods available in the shops. That reaction was soon followed by the statement that Americans must be poor and have no money because the shops had all these desirable but unsold goods. If the Americans had had money, there would not be goods left on the shelves. It took a lot of training and explaining to make them understand how, without the guiding hand of the government, a market economy automatically produces goods for the market and adjusts its production through the impact of price changes on both sellers and buyers, so that, with rare exceptions, goods are always available in the shops.

Returning to the second source of misunderstanding, the "ruble zone," the Soviet Union had been made up of many republics controlled and coordinated by the Communist Party. It used the ruble as its currency. When the Soviet Union broke up in 1991 and new independent states came into existence, some of the policymakers of these states immediately wanted their own central banks to print their own currency in order to assert their economic independence from Russia. However, policymakers from a few countries with closer ties to Russia, which had benefited from the existing economic relations (for example, they were getting cheap energy) wanted to delay this decision. At the time there was a lot of debate on what to do. A much-discussed idea was to establish an economic zone made up of the group of countries in which the ruble would continue to be used. Of course, this required difficult decisions on how to allocate the rubles among these countries and how to control the total amount of rubles created. This zone was labeled the "ruble zone" by Fund economists. The problem arose that in Russian the word zone translates broadly as "concentration camp." Thus, one can imagine the puzzled looks on the faces of former Soviet Union officials when they would hear talks or proposals that implied that the ruble would be placed in a "concentration camp." As it turned out, too many rubles were created leading to high inflation. Thus, the "ruble zone" would come to an end in July 1993.

During these early discussions it became evident that the Russians we met had no understanding of how a market economy operates just as we had little understanding of how a centrally planned economy truly worked. They could not conceive, for example, that there would not be a "price office," an office that would officially set the prices of all goods and services sold in the market, as the Planning Office had done in the Soviet Union. When I was asked at a meeting whether or not the U.S. had a price office, I misunderstood the question and explained that there was an office that kept track of price developments. At this point the Russian officer who had asked the question turned to his colleague sitting next to him and said: "I told you that there is an office in the United States that sets the prices of all products sold!" Obviously they had been debating this question.

Our contacts with Russian officials were always a bit strained at this time. They were still shocked by what had happened to the powerful Soviet Union. Their attitudes reflected the psychology of a people whose country, until the recent chaos, had been considered one of the two world superpowers. Almost overnight they had seen that power vanish and their gross domestic product fall below that of Belgium, measured at the highly devalued, prevailing uncontrolled exchange rate at that time. They had a hard time accepting their new condition and, just like nobles who become paupers within a short span, they resented the foreigners who were now visiting their country to tell them how to run their affairs. To make matters worse, the foreigners represented organizations, such as the IMF and the World Bank, which had been unknown to many of them, because their countries had not been members of these institutions. The fact that these organizations were located in Washington and close to the White House did not help. Some of the Russians we met in these early meetings thought that the IMF was part of the U.S. government and, perhaps, even part of the CIA.

At the Supreme Soviet one of the deputy ministers mentioned that an Italian economist, a communist who had been living in Moscow for decades, had told him that the American economy was also undergoing a great crisis at that time and that it was only a matter of time before it collapsed, as had happened to the economy of the Soviet Union. I tried to explain to him the phenomenon of business cycles, making the point that the U.S. economy in 1991 was undergoing one of its periodic slowdowns but that should not be confused with a breakdown. He did not seem convinced by my explanations and, though courteous, he continued to behave in a way that said: we are a superpower so why are you here? The visit to the tax administration made it clear to us that the Western institution known as the "tax administration" did not exist in Russia, as it had not existed in the Soviet Union. Taxes were, in a basic sense, transfers within different parts of the public sector, normally from the public enterprises to the government proper. The planning office set wages and prices at levels that would generate surpluses in the public enterprises. In this economy, almost all was public sector. Thus, one could not talk about public and private finance. Since there were no "parametric" or objective tax rates stated in tax laws, most of the transfers were the result of negotiations between the managers of the enterprises and officials from what was called the tax administration. Thus, these taxes were largely arbitrary. They often reflected administrative or bureaucratic decisions, not legislation.

Taxes on wages were collected directly from the enterprises that paid net-of-tax wages to the workers. Profit taxes were largely negotiated amounts that did not require the precise measurement of the profits of the enterprises. The profits of the enterprises were normally inflated by the very long economic lives attributed to the capital equipment used. These long lives sharply reduced what in the West are called "depreciation allowances" that reduce taxable profits. In time, the economic lives of the capital assets (the equipment used) were reduced by an average of twenty times and for some by as much as forty times.

These countries had not needed Western-style tax administrators. This was an almost idyllic situation for a "tax administrator." The confrontational situation that often exists in market economies between taxpayers and tax administrators was largely absent. As the director of taxation of one of these countries told me, somewhat nostalgically, in later years, "The life of a tax administrator [during the years of central planning] was easy because of the large size of enterprises." He often had to deal with just one enterprise. "Much revenue came from an occasional telephone call. Now you have to work for every cent." Large enterprises simplified central planning, which facilitated the collection of taxes.

Over the following years, the IMF's Fiscal Affairs Department would play an important role in tax policy and tax administration in Russia. During the decade of transition, the department would help Russia establish a new tax system and a true tax administration. But it would take several years and a lot of hard work on the part of many staff missions. It was also a subject that created significant divisions within the Fund between the tax specialists, who recognized the difficulties of creating an effective tax system and tax administration in a short period of time, and the generalists, who believed that this was an easy or almost trivial objective. These generalists kept assuming that large revenue increases were possible in the short run *if only tax evasion were reduced*! They failed to understand that tax arrears and tax evasion were two different concepts. Tax arrears, which at times reached six percent of GDP in Russia, were largely a form of subsidies that prevented enterprises from going out of business. Tax evasion assumes that those who evade paying the taxes have the means to pay but are not willing to do it. Tax arrears were the result of economic situations in which the enterprises were close to bankruptcy and they would have had to close down and send the workers home if forced to pay the taxes. Policymakers knew the size of the arrears. The problem was a political one that could not be solved by the tax administration. As a result, unrealistic projections of tax revenue made their way into the loan programs negotiated by the IMF with Russia, in spite of strong objections from my department. These unrealistic projections played a significant role in the 1998 Fund program with Russia that, within a month of being signed, was followed by the debacle in which Russia was unable to meet its debt obligations.

The 1991 visit marked the first high level contact between the Fund and the Russian government. I was part of a team of senior staff members headed by Richard Erb, an American, who was then the Deputy Managing Director of the IMF. We were scheduled to meet Yegor Gaidar, who was then Acting Prime Minister of the Russian Federation, and a few other members of the Russian government. They represented a small group of young reformers with some knowledge of market economies. The meeting was to take place in the old headquarters of the Communist Party. The IMF team arrived on time at the building for the scheduled meeting and, through an interpreter, explained to the security guards at the entrance that we had an appointment with Acting Prime Minister Gaidar. The guards had no information about this meeting and were somewhat reluctant to let us in. After some discussion and several telephone calls they allowed us in and told us to take the elevator to a given floor. When we came out of the elevator someone told us to wait in the hallway. There were no chairs there and none were offered. As it was often the case in official buildings in Moscow in December, it was very hot. We were kept waiting for more than one hour. I was getting annoyed and thought that we should leave but Richard Erb, always the patient type, decided that we should wait.

When we were finally invited into a large room, we found the Russian team sitting around a long table. There were introductions but no apologies were offered for having made us wait. Rather, some of them gave us an expression which seemed to imply: why are you here? Gaidar, who at the time was only 35 years of age, was the friendliest of the group, and the fact that he spoke English helped. Erb started to describe the role of the Fund but, while he was talking, Gaidar's attention seemed to be directed toward me. I saw that he was asking a question to Konstantin Kagalovsky, who had been visiting the IMF in the previous months to begin the process of Russia's gaining membership to the Fund. Kagalovsky would become the first Russian Executive Director at the Board of the IMF. At a certain moment Gaidar turned to me and asked whether I was the Tanzi of the "Tanzi effect." I replied that I was, and he asked me to give a brief explanation of that effect. The "Tanzi effect" was caused by the delay in the payment of taxes during a period of high inflation. The longer the delay in the tax payments and the higher the rate of inflation, the greater is the loss in real tax revenue that the government receives. The "Tanzi effect" would play a significant role in Russia in the following years as it had in other countries with high inflation, especially in Latin America. Given the high inflation rate that followed the price liberalization in early 1992, it would contribute to the sharp fall in real tax revenue that made the Russian fiscal situation more difficult in the years immediately after 1991.

When we left this meeting, we went to a location where Erb was scheduled to hold a public press conference. This would be the first press conference by a senior Fund official in Russia. It was, thus, an almost historical event, or at least a significant event. When we got to the building indicated in the address, we found that the main entrance was locked and there was no sign of anyone inside the building. We did not know what to do. After some time someone came and told us that there was a side entrance around the corner of the building which was open. We then managed to enter into a cavernous and poorly lit hall that could have accommodated thousands of people. Unfortunately, there were at most a handful of reporters in the room and nobody else. A reporter from *The Financial Times* asked most of the few, general questions. The whole situation seemed slightly unreal. It did not do justice to this important event, namely Russia joining the Fund and implicitly joining the rest of the World.

I saw Gaidar about a year later at a dinner in Washington when he was no longer prime minister. By this time Viktor Chernomyrdin had been nominated prime minister of Russia. Gaidar had tried to sharply reduce military spending and the size of the Russian military establishment which he considered an essential step in the transition to a market economy and a peaceful, democratic country. At the dinner he complained to me that the West, and especially the United States, had been willing to spend hundreds of billions of dollars for the Cold War but seemed unwilling to spend a few billions to ease the peaceful transition of Russian military personnel to civilian life. This is a mistake that the United Stated would repeat in different parts of the world. In October 1993 there would be an armed uprising in Moscow and an attempt to storm the Russian White House. Gaidar also stated that, in his view, the IMF was the wrong institution for the prominent role it had been given by the leading Western powers in Russia and in other transition countries. The reason he gave was that the IMF was a predominantly macro-economic institution while the changes that Russia needed were more of a structural or institutional nature. The main problem was not macro-economic stabilization, although this was a problem at the time, but institutional transformation. I partly agreed with him. In the fiscal area the IMF did have much more depth than the other international organizations. It was the only international organization with a large, specialized, fiscal department. That department had been created when many former colonies had become free countries, in the 1960s, and had joined the Fund. These new Fund members had needed assistance in creating fiscal and monetary institutions that they had not had. Gaidar was a nice and capable man and one of the true reformers. However, he had tried to change the Russian economy too quickly with a so-called "shock therapy" that may have had too much "shock" and too little "therapy." He died on December 16, 2009 at the still young age of 53.

One evening, I made my first visit to the Red Square with my colleague, Ehtisham Ahmad, a Pakistani economist also from the Fiscal Affairs Department. I recall that it was a very cold night so that there was hardly anyone in the square. However, outside of the Square, just behind the Cathedral of St. Basil, a German rock band, the Scorpions, was giving a rock concert. There were few people attending the concert, and I could not help thinking how incongruous it was for a rock band to play in such a place at this time. I could not help asking myself what Peter the Great, or Lenin, whose mausoleum lay nearby, or Stalin, whose body was also buried a short distance away, would think of this scene. I thought that Lenin and Stalin might, literally, be turning in their graves. I could also visualize the hundreds of Streltsy who had had the temerity to revolt against Peter the Great. As described in Robert K. Massie's Pulitzer price-winning biography *Peter the Great*, the Streltsy were ". . . the shaggy, bearded pikemen and musketeers who guarded the Kremlin and were Russia's first professional soldiers." After being subjected to horrible tortures, the Streltsy were executed and their frozen bodies were left hanging from the walls of the Kremlin for the whole winter. Perhaps the sounds made by the Scorpions would have covered the screams of the prisoners being tortured and executed. The symbolism of the Red Star on one hand and the Scorpions on the other hand was overwhelming. It, perhaps better than any other symbol, indicated that the end of an era had come and that Russia would be different in the future.

Ehtisham and I stood by the concert for a while, braving the cold and absorbing the fantastic sight formed by the Cathedral and by the Walls of the Kremlin. St. Basil's Cathedral or Basilica, completed in 1562, is really extraordinary. It is very different from the Renaissance or Baroque churches that I was accustomed to seeing in Europe or in Latin American countries. From an artistic point of view this "church," that since 1928 ceased to be a church and became a branch of the State Historical Museum, could be from another planet. Its impact on me was somewhat similar to that of the architecture of the royal palaces and the temples of Bangkok or Beijing when I first saw them. We do not fully realize how much of what we consider beautiful, interesting, or even tasty is conditioned by our past experiences. In some way all of us have lived in a well where our brains have absorbed only the impressions of the sights, the objects, the foods, the sounds, and even the smells of what we have been exposed to.

My first reaction to St. Basil's was one of surprise and bewilderment at the strange sight, followed by a growing appreciation for the novel and unusual style. With time I came to appreciate its beauty, especially on sunny days when its multicolored cupolas reflect the rays of the sun. I learned the legend of the two architects, Barna and Postnik, who designed the Cathedral and were blinded after they completed their work, in order to prevent them from building a similar church elsewhere. I could not find out whether this was just a popular legend, or whether it was based on historical facts. I imagine that it is probably just a legend that helps emphasize the unique style of this building. Similar legends have accompanied the creation of other extraordinary buildings, such as the Taj Mahal in India. The Cathedral was built by order of Ivan the Terrible and the body of St. Basil was buried in it in 1588. It was built to commemorate a Russian victory over the Kazan Khanate. On that night of my first visit, a display of fireworks completed the end of the Scorpions' concert, and in the cold and clear night these bursts of light were reflected on the cupolas of the basilica.

The following day, a Sunday, I visited the Kremlin with a couple of colleagues. I learned that the Kremlin had been built by Italian architects in the 15th century. In particular, Ivan III invited Aristotele Fioravanti to plan the complex of the Kremlin. In 1712, another great Russian Tsar, Peter the Great, would invite other Italian architects to build St. Petersburg. The Kremlin has remained the political center of Russia. In front of the main wall of the Kremlin is the Lenin Mausoleum, which contains the embalmed body of Lenin. Furthermore, under the wall are the tombs of other important Russians, such as Stalin and the first man in space, Yuri Gagarin.

We visited several churches within the walls of the Kremlin and admired their magnificent icons. We marveled at a huge bell that, after being built, was found to be too heavy to be carried up on a bell tower. We also admired the engraved ornaments on the cannons left behind by Napoleon, before his retreat from Moscow in 1812. It was hard for me to understand why objects of war, such as cannons, needed to be engraved in such a beautiful way. Maybe artistic beauty was thought to make war more acceptable and less terrible, or to improve the effectiveness of the cannons. Napoleon did not find his Russian adventure a particularly pleasant one. For example, in *1812, Napoleon's Fatal March on Moscow,* Adam Zamoyski describes Napoleon's entry into Moscow. Zamoyski writes that "[Napoleon] was surprised to find no delegation to greet him," as it was customary in those days when a victorious general walked or rode into a conquered city. Rather, the Emperor was greeted by a burning city. This was the end of the summer and the return to France for the Napoleonic army would take place on a territory with little food and progressively colder weather.

The Russian campaign was the turning point in Napoleon's extraordinary life. It was a monumental disaster, certainly one of the greatest military disasters in history. About a million soldiers, fairly divided on both sides, died during this campaign. Some 45,000 Russians and 28,000 on the French side, which included several nationalities, died in the Battle of Borodino alone. The remains of 35,478 horses were later buried by the Russians. Up to the First World War this was, presumably, the most costly battle to date in history, in terms of human lives. However, it should be noted that in ancient times, statistics were not kept.

In addition to churches, our team also visited the famous Gum Department Store, located in front of the Kremlin on Red Square. It had been the pride of Russia. Here the privileged Russians, the so called *nomenklatura*, found goods that the average Russian could never dream of. By Western standards these were hardly luxury shops. However, in a land characterized by scarcity of almost everything, Gum must have looked like heaven to those who had access to it.

At this time Russia was going through a very difficult economic crisis. The old economic system was disintegrating while it would be some time before a new system would be in place. Production had collapsed and, as previously mentioned, food had become very scarce. Many newspaper articles were predicting mass starvation. The streets of Moscow were often lined by vendors—often old ladies but also young men—standing there in the cold for hours trying to sell whatever they could. Much of what they had to offer was really poor stuff. I recall observing an old lady, who seemed to be freezing in the bitter cold, who was offering to sell a single toothbrush. It was a very sad sight. In Arbat Street, the famous Moscow street where art and antiques are sold, impoverished military men trying to earn some rubles would sell products such as military watches and medals of honor. Some watches could only be worn by entitled generals. I bought a few of them for my sons, who still have them and value them. At that time the Russian military were selling almost anything, including planes, tanks, and probably enriched uranium. Some of these items were bought by Chinese, on the frontier between the two countries, in exchange for consumer goods.

We made a point of going into shops and discovering that most of them had empty shelves. Seeing these shops it was easy for us to understand the shock that Russian visitors, and those from other parts of the Soviet Union or from some East European countries, such as Albania, would experience when they first visited some of the shopping malls in Washington, which were overflowing with luxury goods.

On this trip, we had not been provided official cars, as it was often the case during official Fund missions. However, I soon learned, from my colleague Isaias Coelho, that, unlike eating, getting transportation in Moscow was the easiest thing to do. All one had to do was signal to *any* oncoming car and offer one dollar to be taken almost anywhere in Moscow. Most of the time, the offer was quickly accepted. It occurred to me that, at that time, most of the cars one would see in the streets were government cars and the drivers were public employees on some errand during office hours. It was thus, a good bargain for them to earn money by making some detours. Given the black market exchange rate at the time, one U.S. dollar was a large compensation for the service.

Chapter 2

The Bolshevik Experiment

During my 1991 visit to Russia I came to realize how the breakdown of a central planning system and the implementation of a market economy were causing extraordinary distortions in relative prices. There was a point in time when the old economic system had ceased to function but a new system had not yet been introduced. At that point the prices did not have the informational value to consumers and to producers assumed by economists from market economies. I will give below a few examples to convey the extent of the price distortions. On January 1992, as part of the "shock therapy," or the "big bang" strategy, prices would be liberalized and a decision would be made to privatize the public enterprises. However, this latter part of the shock therapy would be implemented a few years later.

With two colleagues, one day we decided to go to the Bolshoi theatre, which was performing one of its famous ballets, Swan Lake. Remarkably the Bolshoi was surviving the economic and political chaos. This was a compliment to the Russian's strong respect for cultural activities, particularly classical dance and music. We walked toward the Bolshoi theatre hoping to be able to buy the tickets. On the way there a young man approached us offering to sell tickets for the night's performance. My colleague Ehtisham Ahmad negotiated the price, and we got three tickets for twelve dollars each. I was sure that the tickets would turn out to be fake. However, when we went to the theatre that evening, they proved to be genuine, although not for particularly good seats. In ruble terms, calculated at the black market exchange rate, we had overpaid by a long shot. However, twelve dollars was a great bargain to us and it would have been difficult and time consuming to get the tickets directly from the ticket office. Most tickets were probably bought by intermediaries, like the young man who had sold them to us, who were willing to stand in line for a long time at the ticket counter. He would make a lot of money selling the dollars in the black market.

When we entered the theatre, well before the time of the performance, we decided to go to the coffee shop inside the theatre. There we purchased a salami and cheese sandwich, a cup of coffee, and a small bag of tangerines which at that time of the year (December) would have been almost impossible to find in the shops of Moscow. The price for each of us for the whole purchase was three American cents! The whole evening had been a great bargain for us because, we enjoyed greatly the performance of Swan Lake, performed with the grace and the technical perfection that have made the Bolshoi one of the world's treasures. We also admired the theatre and the civility of the place.

One evening we were invited to dinner by the then manager of Moscow's McDonald's restaurant, which had been operating in Moscow for about three years. He was a Canadian of Indian origin. He took us to an Indian restaurant that was a joint venture between the city of Moscow and Kerala, an Indian state. The manager of McDonald's was a friend of Satya Poddar, a Canadian also of Indian background, who was a tax consultant working for one of the big accounting firms. Poddar was in Moscow at that time, and I knew him well because he was a member of the International Institute of Public Finance (IIPF). From the manager of McDonald's we learned some interesting facts about this capitalist enterprise in the middle of Moscow. We learned that it was a much bigger operation that one would assume. At that time it hired 1,500 employees and sold about 60,000 hamburgers daily in addition to other items. Given McDonald's strict quality controls on supplies, it must have been very difficult to guarantee the quality under the prevailing circumstances. We learned that it was such a big novelty for Russians to eat at McDonald's that some of them would travel for three or four hours by train just to bring their children to McDonald's for lunch on special occasions. Of course this told us a lot about the relative price of train rides. But I will come back to that.

When our group, including the Canadian host, arrived at the Indian restaurant that evening we entered through a small reception room. This room led to two separate rooms of about the same size. Both of these rooms were part of the same restaurant. The two rooms had identical decor and apparently the same items on the menu. The only difference, and it was a fundamental one, was that the menu of one room had prices in rubles while the menu of the other room had prices in dollars, converted from the ruble prices at the official and widely overvalued exchange rate. At the widely available black market rate the difference in prices for the entries in the two menus was close to one to one hundred. As one would expect, the ruble room was packed and, in spite of the bitter cold, there was a long line outside the restaurant waiting to get in. The room which accepted only payments in dollars was practically empty. One could gain access to the ruble room either through connections, or I presume through bribes, or through very long waits in the cold. The dollar room could be accessed immediately. Thus there was overcrowding in one room and excess capacity in the other. The law of demand was clearly working.

We had the same experience at a Pizza Hut a few nights later. Pizza Hut had recently been introduced in Moscow, and the Russians were developing a fatal attraction for pizza. Here there were also two separate entrances for two rooms, one with prices in dollars and the other prices in rubles. Once again the pizza was the same but the prices were wildly different. Of course, the dollar room was almost empty, while the ruble room had a block-long line of people waiting to get in. Thus we discovered that there was no problem dining out in Moscow as long as one was willing to pay in dollars at the official exchange rate, which made everything very expensive.

The scarcity of food in official shops had created strong incentives for private sector activities. In this period, food production in collective farms had collapsed. However, it had sharply increased in the small pieces of land that workers in collective farms were allowed to cultivate for personal use. Peasants who had small plots of land started to bring food directly to the peasants' markets, which were booming at the time. There was a substantial difference in price between goods sold in official shops and those sold in the peasants' markets. These differences had nothing to do with the exchange rate because in both places the payments were in rubles. The problem was that the official shops could still only sell at the controlled, official prices. Therefore, they were often empty of goods so that, at times, the only available option was the informal peasants' markets. In the peasants' markets, sellers were free to set their own prices. The government indirectly encouraged these markets through the subsidized prices for public transport, and here I am getting back to the question of traveling three or four hours by train just to eat at McDonald's. At that time, a five-hour flight from Moscow to Alma Ata in Kazakhstan cost a little over one U.S. dollar, converted at the black market rate. As a consequence of these absurd prices, peasant women would fly five hours from Alma Ata to Moscow bringing with them a few melons. They would sell them in the peasants' markets and receive enough money to cover the plane ticket and make a good profit.

A major contribution to the price distortion was the absurd pricing of energy. Russia is a country rich in energy resources, such as oil and natural gas, and the Soviet Union's policy had been to consider energy almost a free good. At the time I was in Moscow, gasoline prices were very low. As a consequence, there was a lot of unnecessary energy use. For every million dollar of GDP produced, the Soviet Union was using several times as much energy as other countries. This waste of energy could be seen everywhere. Apartments and buildings were generally overheated, and in the winter Muscovites would often control the temperature in their apartments by opening and closing their windows.

An extreme example of the Soviet attitude vis-à-vis the use—or better the waste—of energy was the very large *outdoor* swimming pool that was *open year-round*, even during the bitterly cold Russian winters. This large pool was heated so that the citizens of Moscow could enjoy it while the outside temperature might have been 20 or 30 degrees below zero! As an obvious political statement, the pool had been built on the site where the main Basilica of the Russian Orthodox Church had stood for centuries. Stalin, in 1931, had the Basilica destroyed. He had wanted to destroy all the churches but was fortunately dissuaded from completely carrying out his project. Many churches were destroyed. Others were transformed into museums or converted to other uses, so that the buildings survived in these other functions.

In the 1990s the Mayor of Moscow rebuilt the Basilica, replacing the pool. The project cost an enormous amount of money, apparently some six-hundred million dollars. All the money was reportedly "donated" by individuals and enterprises. However, rumors circulated that the Mayor made requests that could not be refused because of his tremendous regulatory power over economic activities in Moscow. The new Basilica has magnificent mosaics and paintings and is certainly worth visiting. Though the Muscovites lost their place to swim all year around, they gained one where they could pray all year around. Russia saved a lot of energy in the process and reestablished its relation with God. Religion got its revenge over communism. Still today, the domestic prices of natural gas or petroleum are a fraction of the price at which Russia exports gas and petroleum.

Returning to the availability of food and the distortion in prices, there were some unusual aspects that I could not explain. For example, milk and sugar were hard to find individually. At the same time ice cream, which requires both, was widely available and very cheap. Pensions had fallen to two or three dollars per month, and most salaries were around five to six dollars a month at the black market rate. At the same time our hotel rooms were three-hundred U.S. dollars a night, and the taxi fare to the airport was sixty dollars. That was about ten months' salary for the average Russian. The same jar of caviar could be bought in the streets of Moscow for eight dollars, at the airport shop for one hundred and sixty dollars, and, as I found out during my return trip, in Budapest for twenty-eight dollars. Clearly the law of one price, implicit in an efficient market, had not established itself for this product. I bought some nice paintings, representing scenes from the peasants' markets, and paid nine dollars for each of them.

As would be expected in such a situation there were many ladies of the night. They were especially present in the hotel, or more specifically, at each floor of the hotel. Coming out of the elevators an attractive girl, often with long legs and blond hair, would approach you and ask if you had a light. The question was followed by another one: would you like company? The hotel management seemed largely indifferent to these activities. I presume that they shared in the proceeds of what must have been a profitable activity.

When I left Moscow, it was snowing and the road was very slippery. There were few cars on the road but a high proportion of them were driven by individuals who had had too many drinks. This was obvious by the way the cars were driven. The preferred drink in Russia is Vodka, often bad Vodka. Drinking had become a big or a bigger problem in Russia and this risk, combined with other health risks (high pollution, stress, poor diet, and a poor healthcare system) made Russia one of the few countries in the world with a declining life expectancy. Gorbachev had attempted to reduce drinking but without much success. As of today, 2010, life expectancy for male Russians is only fifty-nine years, at least 15 years below that of Western European countries. For both men and women it is 66 years down from 69.2 years in the 1990s. Because of this phenomenon, Russia is less likely to have major problems associated with the aging of the population.

Whether we realize it or not, we often have some preconceived notions, or even feelings, of particular places that we have never visited but about which we have often heard in the news. During the long years of the Cold War, Russia had been in the news a great deal, especially in countries exposed to the danger of Communist takeover. In Italy, where I had been living before I moved to the

United States in 1956, Russia had been the reference point for the Italian Communist Party. That Party presented Russia as a kind of paradise for the working classes, a place where the state would eventually vanish and the working classes would have direct control over their lives and would live happily after. The Russian Communist Party used this idealization to justify the prohibition of strikes in Russia because, they argued, it would not make sense for workers to strike against themselves. However, outside of Russia strikes were a powerful tool for the working classes and were often instigated by Communist parties. The Soviet system was presented as the inevitable, historically determined future of the world. Brainwashed visitors to Russia would say: "we have seen the future and it works." They would argue that only ignorance could prevent one from seeing the "obvious" moral and economic superiority of a world in which private property would disappear and society would provide each person with all the necessities of life. All the economic risks that exist for individuals in a market economy would disappear because the state would take care of them and there would not be any class distinction or any poor people. As they would put it: "from each according to his ability and to each according to his needs." Thus, the able would support the needy. The four wise men of communism, Marx, Engels, Lenin, and Stalin had done a good job of promoting this Utopian possibility.

When I was a high school student in Italy in the 1950s, the country was a cauldron of competing ideologies. Even though Mussolini's fascist regime had been overthrown the previous decade, fascism was still present as an ideology. I recall some of my schoolteachers as being openly nostalgic about the fascist period, which they associated with law and order, trains that arrived on time, respect for family values, and pride in the country. Democratic ideas, pushed mainly by the dominant Christian Democratic Party, were acquiring a large following and reflected the views of the Christian-democratic government that was in power at that time. However, the Italian Communist Party, the largest such party in Western Europe, was very powerful and generally got the votes of about one third of the Italian electorate. While the Christian Democratic Party relied on the Catholic Church for support, the leftist parties relied on intellectuals who, in Italy as well as in other European countries at that time, had often leftist tendencies. The movies—in the *realismo* style—and much of the literature at that time had a leftist bent. The Communist Party expected it would replace the Christian Democratic Party in the government at some point and was working hard at promoting its ideology. The leftist parties, which included the Communists as well as some far-left socialists parties, that wanted an expanded role of the state in the economy and the nationalization of most large enterprises (but not the abolishment of all private property or activities) had made large inroads among Italian intellectuals and among workers in industrial enterprises. They were trying hard to promote their ideas among the young and especially among students. Students would argue for hours about these ideas with little factual knowledge but with a lot of passion. I recall participating in discussions in which some members of the leftist parties, generally students who were just a few years older than the rest of us, described for us the paradise that the Russian Communist Party was creating in the Soviet Union.

I recall that one time these members read from a Russian book that in Italian was called *Che Fare?* (*What Is to Be Done?*). In this book the author, Nikolai Chernyshevsky, described a workers' paradise. In this "paradise" children would be taken away from their mothers a short time after their birth and would be raised communally with a tutor assigned to them and with violinists awakening them in the morning with the sound of beautiful classical music. In this utopia the workers would be the masters. I recall asking the speaker the impertinent but inevitable question that came to my practical mind: "who would pick up the garbage in that society?" "Who would cook and clean the dishes?" My practical mind could not fail to see the system described in the book, which had been outlined by the speaker, for what it was: a utopia, not something that could really exist. I was puzzled that some of my friends, whom I considered very smart, would believe in that nonsense. Some of these people remained true believers until the Stalinist era's atrocities, namely the millions of Russians killed between 1937–1938, or those who had died during the first Five Year Plan of 1928, came to light after Stalin's death in 1953. At that time the Italian Communist Party distanced itself from its Russian counterpart but its ideology did not really change. I later learned, from Martin Amis's book *Koba the Dread: Laughter and the Twenty Million*, that Lenin had read the Chernyshevsky book five times in one summer and that the novel had "completely reshaped" Lenin's life. Amis's conclusion is that this book was "the most influential novel of all time." It is easy to agree with him because no other novel has ever had such an impact on the world.

Seeing what was happening in Russia at the time of my visit, I developed a great curiosity about the Communist period and about how an intelligent people, as are the Russians, had allowed itself to be taken for such an incredible ride. Within the limited time that I had available, I started reading several books on Stalin and on the period. I was astonished to read that between August 1937, when the Great Terror started, and November 1938, about 700,000 people were executed. This comes to about 2,000 a day, or 83 per hour. Furthermore, another 300,000 died during interrogations that were always accompanied by torture. Stalin himself, an individual who had received a seminary education in Georgia and who wrote poetry and liked singing, had instructed the head of the secret service on how to conduct the interrogations. His instruction had been simple and to the point: "hit, hit, and hit even more" until those being questioned admitted to the absurd crimes of which they had been accused. Thus, the famous law of torture to get to the "truth" was in full force. What I found truly frightening was that these executions had been conducted in full observance of the "rule of law." The arrests, trials, convictions, and executions had respected Soviet laws and full records had been kept of them. In some cases, those tortured or questioned seemed disposed to admit to crimes that they had *not* committed when they believed that their "confessions" would help the Communist Party in its historical mission. Somehow I could see a lot of similarity between these actions and those of religious martyrs who sacrificed themselves with the belief that this would promote the goals of their faith. Arthur Koestler, a former Communist, masterfully captured the psychology of such individuals in his book, *Darkness at Noon*. This book had been inspired by the trial of Nikolai Bucharin, who had been a member of the Politburo and who had confessed to crimes that he had not committed and had called for his own execution.

In 2000, a book published in Italy called *Diario della Moglie di un Bolscevico* (*Diary of a Bolshevik Wife*) caught my attention. It was the diary of Julia Pyatnizkaya, the wife of Osip Pyatnizky, a devout Bolshevik, who had spent his life for the cause. He was arrested and executed in 1938. His crime was that he had spoken against initiating the Great Terror, which would give full powers to the secret police, at a meeting with Stalin. At this time one could be arrested and shot for being the first to stop applauding after a speech by Stalin. This created a strong incentive to keep applauding and, for sure, guaranteed long applauses. In time a signal would indicate when to stop. Julia

Pyatnizkaya's book is the diary she kept after her husband's arrest and before she herself was arrested. She and their sixteen-year-old son were arrested a few months after Osip and were sent to Siberia for the serious crimes of being his wife and son. She died in the Gulag during the Great Terror. What makes this book so interesting is that the wife, who is also a convinced Communist, knows that the husband cannot be guilty and that he has dedicated all his life to the Communist movement. However, she also cannot accept that the Party might be wrong and keeps thinking, up to the end, even after she is herself arrested, that the husband must have done something of which she was unaware. It is difficult to understand the Soviet experiment without understanding the almost religious fanaticism that accompanied it. This helps explain why Stalin still has a significant *following* in Russia. There are still some true believers left especially among older individuals. It is still common today to see people, normally old people, occasionally demonstrating in favor of Stalin near the Kremlin.

Another book that helped me understand how the Soviet experiment could have happened was also a small book, *Nella Russia dei Soviet* (*In the Russia of the Soviets*), which I also read in its Italian version. The book is a compilation of articles written by a famous French reporter, Albert Londres, who in 1920 managed to get a visa to visit Moscow after months of failed attempts. At the time of Londres's visit, several Western intellectuals tended to close their eyes to what was happening in Russia. But very few, most of whom were already sympathizers, were taken on carefully controlled tours when allowed to visit Russia. Londres seems to have immediately grasped what the Soviet regime was about, and his observations were remarkably perceptive and to the point.

What I found particularly interesting were the interviews he conducted with the foreign affairs commissar (Minister of Foreign Affairs) and with the finance commissar (Minister of Finance). These were held at the hotel Metropol, which in 1920 had been commissioned to be the Ministry of Foreign Affairs and the Ministry of Finance. Londres was particularly happy when he received authorization to visit the Ministry of Foreign Affairs and interview the minister. He writes that at that time one needed permission "even to look up at the sky." The person bringing the permit tells Londres that the meeting will take place at 3:00 a.m. on a specific day. Londres corrects him that he must mean 3:00 p.m., but he is told that the time is, in fact, 3:00 a.m. In the middle of a cold night,

Londres walks through the streets of Moscow where he sees many emaciated, starving, and freezing people already waiting in line for the horrible bread that they will get in the morning that will keep them alive a bit longer. He hears some shots that he assumes indicate, for some people, a departure from this to the other world, courtesy of representatives of the regime in power.

At exactly 3:00 a.m., Londres is shown into the Office of the Minister, or better of Comrad Chicherin. It is a hotel room, large and messy but almost devoid of furniture. Londres observes that the mess reminds him of the "*marché au puce*" (the flea or thieves' market) in Paris. The Minister, who has lived in this room the whole winter without any heating, is wearing two overcoats. He sleeps during the day and works at night. He is an ascetic, originally from a noble family, but a true believer with perfect Bolshevik credentials. He has elegant manners, inherited from his noble background, and he receives Londres courteously. He explains that the sole goal of the Soviets is the happiness of the Russian people and that the Soviets are creating a workers' paradise, as it should be obvious to any well-meaning and perceptive person. As the conversation with Chicherin unfolds, Londres observes, "a mistake that a visitor to Moscow cannot commit is to consider Bolshevism as a political party. It is not a political party, but an order of monks" (my translation). He follows with the observation that: "The French Revolution had proclaimed the rights of man; the Bolshevik revolution proclaims the rights of the State on man."

John Maynard Keynes, the famous economist, had similar observations to those of Londres after his visit to Russia, during his honeymoon in 1925. Keynes had married the Russian classic ballerina Lydia Lopokova on August 4, 1925 and had gone to Leningrad to meet her parents in September. He had traveled also to Moscow. When he returned to England, he referred to the religiosity of Leninism and to the inefficiency of the new system being set up.

In Londres's book, I found a second interview especially illuminating because of its economic content. It takes place between Londres and the Minister of Finance, still at the hotel Metropol, in room No. 423 to be precise. The Minister informs him that one of the regime's objectives is the "elimination of money" from society. For this reason, "his greatest joy was to see the ruble lose value every day." After this observation, Londres asks the minister: "Suppose that I need a hat, what can I do Mr. Minister?"

"Simple: You will bring your need to the president of the committee of the place where you live, get a certificate from him, and go to the communal house of hats to receive your hat."

"What if the president of the committee (for whatever reason) refuses?"

The minister just smiles without answering. Londres asks another question: "What if money has been abolished but one needs to go abroad?"

"Why?" asks the Minister.

"For no particular reason."

"Then, he would not go... The Republic of workers will not need Russians that go around without reasons." In fact freedom of movement within Russia (or within China) was abolished during Communist time. These and other priceless exchanges can be found in this marvelous little book.

Reading Londres's book helped me understand, in a truly fundamental sense, what had happened in Russia from 1920 to 1990. The main change over this time was that the incorruptible "religious" fanatics who initiated the Communist movement were progressively replaced by corrupt cynics who brought it to an end. These were the ones described in David Remnick's Pulitzer Prize winning book, *Lenin's Tomb: The Last Days of the Soviet Empire*. Remnick described the extent to which corruption had metastasized in the Soviet System by the 1980s. By Brezhnev's time, even getting a dead body accepted into a morgue required a bribe. Nobody visited Brezhnev without bringing gifts. Among these three wonderful books, Albert Londres's book could be the first chapter of that seventy years' tragedy. Julia Pyatnizkaya's book could be considered an intermediate chapter, with David Remnick's book as the concluding chapter. What remains to be seen is how those seventy years will affect the future of Russia. For this we will have to wait. For sure there will be an economic and a political transition. These transitions are still in progress with perhaps the economic one having progressed more than the political one.

The experience of the Communist period undoubtedly had major economic consequences. It started with the aim of suppressing money, and even the laws of economics, and ended with a period in which a country rich in natural resources, in land, and with a very able population, risked starvation. Amis cites the Party economist, S.C. Strumilin, who during the period of forced collectivization (1929–1933) had said that: "Our task is not to study economics but to change it. We are bound by no [economic] law." In the attempt to change economics they had created what Wassily Leontief called a peculiar "input-input" system. Leontief was a Nobel Prize winner in economics who had been raised in Russia before emigrating to the U.S. In this "input-input" system, resources went into the system, but nothing of real value came out of it. In other words, the Soviet economic system became a kind of black hole that absorbed enormous capital and human resources and produced few, useful consumption goods. Leontief had won the Nobel Prize in Economics for developing "input-output analysis," which is the analysis of the relation between the inputs used by an economic system and the output in terms of useful goods that it produces. A very colorful man, Leontief had been one of my professors at Harvard.

The next chapter will focus on the decade of the 1990s when the International Monetary Fund assisted the Russian government in the difficult task of transforming the command economy in which all significant economic decisions are "commands" by the policymakers to one in which free individuals spontaneously make those decisions.

Chapter 3

Russia: When the IMF Danced with the Bear

In 1992, the Russian economy would see many changes under President Yeltsin and Prime Minister Gaidar. In September of that year, in collaboration with the Austrian government, the IMF, the World Bank, the OECD, the European Commission, and the newly-created European Bank for Reconstruction and Development (EBRD) opened a training center in Vienna for officials from transition economies. The Vienna Center would train officials from those countries to initiate and carry out institutional and policy reforms that the countries needed to become market economies. The IMF would provide most of the instructors while the Austrian government would provide the physical facilities. The Center would share space with the Austrian Customs School that, as a result of various historical developments (dissolution of the Austro-Hungarian Empire, the creation of the European Union), had excess capacity. Vienna was considered an ideal location for the training center because during the cold war it had been a kind of frontier town between the centrally-planned countries of the East and the market-oriented countries of the West.

Michel Camdessus, then the Managing Director of the IMF, had been a driving force in the creation of this center. He saw it as a kind of World University where East would meet West. He pushed for a large role in the transition for the IMF, an institution that was able to move quickly when needed.

The official opening of the Vienna Center was an important political event. Some of the attendees included: the President of Austria; various Austrian Ministers; the Governor of the Austrian Central Bank; the heads of the IMF, the OECD, and the EBRD; and high level representatives of the World Bank and the European Commission. The heads of the IMF, the OECD, and the EBRD were Camdessus, Paye, and Attali, respectively. The representatives of the World Bank and of the European Commission were Mr. Talwitz and Mrs. Scrivener. The opening ceremony took place at the Austrian President's official residence in the same room where the Treaty of Vienna was signed in 1815, the treaty that would try to bring stability and peace to Europe after the Napoleonic wars.

The creation of the Center and the formal opening had created some frictions among the various institutions. Problems arose related, in particular, to the financing the Center, to the specific roles that each institution would play, and to the transition in general. The breakup of the Soviet Union came to be seen as a major historical development, and each institution wanted to play a major role in the process of transition. Other institutions, inevitably, resented the IMF's prominent role. That resentment would create some continuing difficulties in successive years.

At the Center's opening there had been some discussion as to who would speak first and who would be the first signatory of the formal documents. The friction was intensified by the fact that the heads of the IMF, the OECD, and the EBRD all happened to be French, with inevitable rivalries. Alan Whittome, then the British director of the European Department at the IMF, diplomatically tried to find acceptable solutions. At this time Jacques Attali, the head of the EBRD, was under intense attacks, especially by the British press, for excessive expenditures, such as hiring a French chef, decorating the EBRD headquarter in London with expensive marble, and for spending a lot of money on the logo design for the EBRD. At this time the OECD was in search of a more important role to justify its existence, while the European Commission could not decide what it should do. As it turned out, the European Commission assumed a mostly financing role. Perhaps the fact that the Fund, rather than the World Bank, would be the main institution engaged in guiding the transition may have shifted the attention from institution-building to policy because the Fund was the prominent institution especially with respect to macro-economic policy. However, in the fiscal and central banking areas the Fund had had, traditionally, considerable depth, because it had large departments dealing with these issues.

Some of the above-mentioned frictions were related to what the various institutions should do (a) at the Austrian training center, (b) vis-à-vis Eastern European countries, and (c) in the countries that had come into existence out of the breakup of the Soviet Union. Over the next several years there would be continuous frictions, especially vis-à-vis the World Bank, and several attempts at smoothing things over. For a while, in the earlier years, Mr. Grigory Yavlinsky, an economic adviser to Mr. Gorbachev, would relate the requests coming from the Russian government. In 1990 he had collaborated with Stanislav Shatalin, a well-known Russian economist who was an adviser to Gorbachev, in developing a 500-Day Plan that would transform the Soviet economy into a market economy. Strong Communist opposition to the Plan had led to its abandonment and Yavlinsky would soon disappear from the group of main actors.

The Center's first training seminar had been scheduled immediately after the official opening ceremony. Because of this it was attended by several high-level officials from Former Soviet Union (FSU) countries that had been invited to the opening. Senior staff members of the IMF had been sent to Vienna to lecture at that first seminar. They included Manuel Guitian, a well-regarded Spanish economist with a Chicago Ph.D., who would speak on currency boards; Guillermo Calvo, a well-known Argentine economist, now a Professor at Colombia University, who would speak on Latin American experiences with stabilization policies; and myself who would discuss fiscal policy.

At this point in time there was, perhaps, too much emphasis on "policies" and not enough on "institutions," perhaps not realizing that institutions are the vehicles that carry the policies. If the right institutions do not exist, as they did not exist at that time in most of the centrally-planned countries, the discussion of policies could appear abstract to the participants and some "good" policies could have perverse short run effects. This conflict, between discussions of policies and the need to create the institutions, would continue for several years, both between institutions (the World Bank and the IMF) and within the IMF (between the Fiscal Affairs Department and the Central Banking department, on one hand, and some other departments, on the other hand). For example what effect could a shock therapy (freeing of prices and privatization) have on an economy without the essential institutions to respond to price changes and to allow an honest process of privatization? Could prices be freed given the large amount of rubles (the monetary overhang) in the hands of citizens? An original early idea was to absorb the ruble overhang with privatization. But could privatization be implemented without the essential institutions for it?

The first regular course in public finance for a larger group of participants, a course that lasted six weeks and was directed toward mid-level officials, was organized in April 1993. At that time the rooms where the participants would be staying were still being prepared. On the opening day of the course a logistic problem had developed. Some of those from the FSU countries who had been invited to attend the course had arrived at the airport of Vienna without any Austrian money to pay for the taxis that would take them to the Training Center. The Austrian police had to intervene and help them transfer to the Center. The participants turned out to be a bunch of lively and articulate individuals. What they missed in knowledge of market economies they made up in enthusiasm and intelligence. I was surprised by their general cultural sophistication even by those from Albania that had been a very closed country, resembling North Korea today. Some of them even spoke Italian. They had learned it by watching Italian television programs!

We tried to introduce them to how a market economy functioned, to the concept of taxes, fiscal deficits, and others. Most of them had never paid taxes because the taxes on their wages had been directly transferred from the public enterprises to the government and wages were their sole income. The taxes were calculated on the total wage bill of the enterprise. The concept of fiscal deficit was also alien to them because it requires a clear separation between the private and the public part of an economy. This separation was artificial in these countries, where all had been public. Furthermore, concepts of safety nets to protect citizens against some risks with economic consequences, such as illnesses, unemployment, etc. were also alien to them. The whole government activity had been a safety net during communist times. Those who attended the courses participated actively in the discussion but much was lost in translation, even when they spoke English, because many words had different meanings for us and for them. By this time the institutions (and the policies) that had existed under central planning were being dismantled but those that would in time replace them were not yet in place. An institutional vacuum had appeared. It would take several years to create the needed institutions. During those years the fiscal situation would deteriorate in all of these countries and, by forcing the governments to print money to finance their expenses, would contribute to high inflation and sharp falls in output. In 2003, Chernomyrdin became prime minister, the ruble zone was dissolved, and the International Monetary Fund reached an agreement with Russia on a Systemic Transformation Facility, a program that would help Russia both financially and technically during the period when the Russian economy would be transformed in a market economy.

While in Vienna I was invited to give a seminar at the Central Bank of Austria. The seminar was on the economic transformation that was taking place. It was well attended and well received. I met the Governor of the Central Bank (a lady) who, at that time, was the best paid governor of central banks in the world. Her salary and the salaries of the bank employees were under attacks and were creating some political problems for the government. In time the salaries would be brought more in line with those of other, similar countries.

I was invited by the officials of the central bank to go to the Vienna Opera House where I saw *Tosca*, accompanied by one of the officials. The Opera House had been badly damaged during the Second World War and restored after the war but it was still very beautiful. I was impressed by the elegance of those attending the opera and grateful for the invitation I had received. I was, thus, somewhat amused when, a couple weeks later, back in Washington, I got the rather expensive bill for my opera ticket!

By this time the IMF was fully engaged in Russia and was being pushed by various governments, and especially by the American government, to be even more active in Russia and in other "transition economies." We were continually reminded that Russia still had thousands of atomic bombs. At that time a stream of Fund economists and outside consultants on particular areas (tax administration, budget, statistics, central banking, etc.) hired by the Fund had started the complicated and difficult process of helping transform "centrally planned or command economies" into "market economies." This transformation would require new policies and especially new institutions and the drastic transformation of some existing ones. An office was opened by the Fund in Moscow with a significant number of Fund economists. Also the staff of the IMF was significantly expanded to be able to accommodate the additional work created by some 30 countries that had joined the IMF, as new members, and that needed a lot of assistance. Each of these countries needed much technical assistance and each would receive a yearly Fund mission that would write a lengthy report, as required by the Article IV of the IMF charter. For a couple of years the IMF became the major employer in the world of new Ph.D.s in economics graduating from major universities. Unfortunately most of the Fund economists, or for that matter most of the Western economists, had little knowledge of the way centrally planned economies had worked. This knowledge was badly needed to assist the countries make a successful transition.

Both within the IMF and outside of it, two schools of thought had developed on how to achieve the ultimate goal of a market economy in the new members of the IMF. On one hand there were those, especially among individuals trained largely as macroeconomists, who represented the majority of the Fund staff, who believed that the transition to a market economy needed mostly or mainly two *policies*: the liberalization of prices and the privatization of state enterprises. Enact these two policies and, *voilá*, as by magic, formerly centrally planned economies would wake up the next morning as market economies. This was a kind of "Big Bang" theory or "Shock Therapy." The proponents of this method were individuals trained largely as macroeconomists. They included some well-known economists both within and outside the IMF. Many leading economists stressed the need for a rapid privatization of enterprises.

On the other hand there were the realists or the so-called structuralists, who believed that the transition process should be more gradual and would require a lot of time and effort because it needed not just the change in some policies but the creation of public *and private* institutions that had not existed in the centrally planned economies. The public institutions included a tax system, a tax administration, a budget office, a treasury, a relatively independent central bank, a good statistical office, and regulators to enforce market behavior in various areas. The needed private institutions included insurance companies, stock exchanges, etc. To create these institutions, it would take much time and effort. Essential skills such as those of lawyers, accountants, financial agents, real estate agents, and so on were also needed. Some of these skills had not existed or had been very scarce in centrally planned economies. Thus, the realists believed, the transition would be inevitably lengthy and messy.

In those years I edited and contributed to two books on issues related to public finance in transition economies. One, *Fiscal Policies in Economies in Transition*, was published in 1992. The other, *Transition to Market: Studies in Fiscal Reform* was published in 1993. The contributors to these books were, for the most part, experts from the Fiscal Affairs Department of the IMF who were then engaged in providing technical assistance to the authorities of the countries in transition and who were aware of the difficulties. The two books were published by the IMF, in English, Russian, and Chinese editions. One of them, *Transition to Market* won a book prize. During later years I occasionally met officials from the former Soviet Republics, East European countries, and China who mentioned that these books had been useful to them because they had dealt in realistic ways with real issues of immediate concerns to them. The books had provided some practical, even though not always correct, guidance on what to do in certain areas.

In the first half of the 1990s the gap in understanding on what to do, between the IMF staff, on one hand, and, especially, the Russians on the other hand, and between the macroeconomists and the realists or, better, the structuralists, was particularly wide. The fiscal situation had deteriorated in most of the transition countries. The economic advice being given did not seem to be producing the expected and desired results. There were enormous drops in the measured gross domestic products of most of these countries (in some of them by more than 50 percent) and sharp increases in measured fiscal deficits. Fiscal deficits, as conventionally measured, seemed to fluctuate widely partly because of the effect of inflation and the difficulties in taking it into account in the measurement of the deficit. This led me to write a paper, published by the Fund *Staff Papers*, the official, academic publication of the IMF, warning about the interpretation or the meaning of these deficits. (December 1993). I argued that real fiscal deficits probably were fluctuating much less than the measured ones. Inflation was accelerating in most of these countries, because of central bank financing of public spending and because of the removal of controls on prices.

At this time we ran into strange theories that showed the extent to which our Russian counterparts, regardless of their intelligence, and some of them were clearly *very* smart, had a hard time to understand how market economies operate. It should be recalled that central planning had dominated the Russian economy for more than 70 years. Thus, there were no Russians with still some memory of how a market economy operated. This was a different situation from China where the Communist dogma had dominated for less than 30 years, before it began to be abandoned. In China in the late 1970s and 1980s there were still many people who had been adults in the 1940s and had some memories of market economies. Perhaps, this may help explain why the transition process, still to be completed, has been so much more successful and smooth in China. Part of that process was described in my book, *Peoples, Places and Policies: China, Japan and Southeast Asia* (2008).

To return to the theories which I mentioned regarding the Russian transition, I will note two strange ones, both advanced by some of the more clever Russian officials that I encountered. The first one, proposed by one of the Deputy Ministers of Finance, argued that an expansion of the supply of money would reduce the velocity of money and, thus, inflation. The assumption was that when people have more money available, they do not need to use it as quickly as when they have less money available, thus slowing down its velocity. In this view monetary scarcity forces people to spend the money they have more quickly. Obviously this person had no understanding of the fact that, as more money is created, the ratio between money available and goods produced increases so that prices go up unless they are controlled. If the prices are controlled, the increase in money leads to long lines and empty shelves. Only in particular circumstances would the increase in money lead to an increase in output and a fall in prices. He was obviously confusing the creation of money with an increase in real income, believing that the creation of money automatically created real income and real output.

Another theory, reported in an article in *Izvestia*, the leading Russian newspaper, argued that inflation could be reduced by cutting the already very low price of oil. It should be recalled that the price of oil in Russia at that time was only a very small fraction of world prices. The argument was that the simple announcement that the price of oil had been cut would convince the Russian public that inflation was coming down. Thus, the change in expectations would reduce prices immediately. I found this theory so strange that I sent the *Izvestia* article to the *Journal of Political Economy*, the economic journal published at the University of Chicago. This journal carried a special feature on its back page reporting strange and weird economic theories. The journal agreed with my assessment of the theory and published the *Izvestia* article! Thus the author of that theory could claim, on his curriculum vitae, an article in the prestigious *Journal of Political Economy*!

The role of the IMF in Russia became increasingly controversial, both in Moscow and in Washington. For example at a press conference in Moscow, then Vice President Al Gore blamed the Fund and the World Bank for the election result of December 12, 1993. The elections had given 23 percent of the votes in the State Duma to the nationalist party of Vladimir Zhirinovsky. It had been assumed that harsh conditions imposed by the IMF had contributed to this result. Gore stated that the Fund had been slow in recognizing the political consequences of the conditions that it imposed on countries, when they borrowed from the IMF. This was a common criticism of the IMF at that time. Of course, as was often the case, the Fund was being blamed for sins that it had committed and for sins that it had not. As someone put it, he who wants to play the role of the ringmaster, must take the blame for the behavior of the lions. Definitely, willing or not, the Fund had assumed the role of ringmaster.

A joke that circulated at the time in Moscow captures the essence of how Russians saw the relationship between the IMF and Russia. A peasant farmer had gone to see a veterinarian and had explained to him that he was raising rabbits but the rabbits were dying at an unusually high rate. The veterinarian advised the farmer to change the feed that he was giving to the rabbits. The farmer left but a few weeks later he came back to see the veterinarian, explaining that he had followed his advice but the rabbits were still dying at the same high rate. The veterinarian thought for a while and concluded that if the cause for the high mortality of the rabbits was not the feed that they were getting, it must be the space they had available. Therefore, he recommended that the rabbits be given more space. The farmer left but a few weeks later he returned and told the veterinarian that he had given more space to the rabbits but they were still dying at the same high rate. At this point the veterinarian suggested that if the normal, traditional remedies (feed and space) were not working, new remedies, requiring more imagination and more expertise, were needed. He explained that recent research had shown that rabbits needed to be entertained. Furthermore, they seemed to respond well to classical music, especially to the music of Mozart or Tchaikovsky. He advised the farmer to entertain the rabbits by playing some good classical music for them. The farmer looked a bit puzzled but left to follow the expert's advice. A few weeks later he returned and told the veterinarian that he had followed his latest advice but all the rabbits had died. The veterinarian's reaction was immediate: "what a pity; I had so many other good ideas!" Fairly or unfairly the Russians saw the Fund as the veterinarian and the Russian economy as the peasant farmer. Of course once the Fund had entered the Russian scene it could not disengage itself regardless of developments. As some Russians put it at that time, "once you start dancing with a bear, it is the bear that decides when to stop."

Both sides were suffering from some kind of naïveté. On the Fund side, there was the belief that policies that work in market economies would work in an economy such as Russia, which was fundamentally different in its institutional set up and was run by individuals who were still entrenched in their own past knowledge and past experience. As the famous French historian Fernand Braudel once put it: "opinions are long term prisons." On the Russian side some had accepted the notion that a market economy would automatically solve many economic problems, even when the transition to such a market, especially in the earlier years, was more rhetorical than real. At times I had the feeling that in Russia, everything had changed but nothing had changed, at least in a fundamental way. In *The Leopard*, the famous book written by the Prince of Lampedusa, the same observation was made about Sicily during the Italian unification and the occupation by the Piemontese forces. Once again a joke that circulated in Moscow captured the essence of the problem. The joke began with a question: how many people it takes to replace a burned-out light bulb. The answer was: in a centrally planned economy it takes four, one to screw the bulb and three to keep a record of the action. In a market economy nobody is needed, because the market, or an invisible hand, will do it!

These were the years that preceded the so called "nomenklatura" or "loans for share" privatization when well connected individuals managed to acquire great wealth by stripping state enterprises of their most valuable assets, at fire sales prices, or by buying, at ridiculously low prices, the shares distributed to the population in a program of mass privatization. The announcement of the voucher privatization had been made by Yeltsin on August 14, 1992 but "the loans for share privatization" would start at the end of 1995. It would be led by Anatoly Chubais. Within a few years, a country that had not had rich people, and where income equality had been the goal, ended up with some of the wealthiest individuals on Earth. For a fascinating account of the meteoric rise of one of these oligarchs see Paul Klevnikov, *Godfather of the Kremlin: Boris Berezovsky and the Looting of Russia* (2000). As Klebnikov put it: "In just ten years Berezovsky transformed himself from a scientist researching decision-making theory into Russia's most successful deal maker . . . who went on to seize control of some of Russia's largest companies." In April 2004, *Forbes Russia* reported that 36 individuals living in Moscow were billionaires in U.S. dollars. Considering that in the whole world the estimated number of billionaires in 2004 was about 600, this was an extraordinary number. This number for Moscow was higher than for any other city in the world. The reporter that had helped establish *Forbes Russia* would be murdered. *Forbes's* March 26, 2007 *Special Issue* would raise the number of Russia's billionaires to 53 with a combined net worth of U.S. $282 billion. Russia was then third among countries in the number of billionaires, just behind Germany. In 2008, there would be 7 Russians among the

30 richest individuals in the world and Russia's richest 100 people would all be billionaires (see *Forbes Russia* 2008). The 2008–2009 economic crisis would reduce significantly that number. Bloomberg reported that during the first five months of the 2008 financial crisis Russian billionaires lost $230 billion. However by 2010 the number of billionaires in Russia would rise to 62. See *Forbes*, Special Edition of April 26, 2010.

The issue of property rights, acquired through potentially legal means but means considered illegitimate by much of the Russian population, would come to haunt the market economy that was being created in Russia; perhaps, even its democracy. It would be used by Putin, whose grandfather had cooked for Stalin, and who had succeeded Yeltsin as President of Russia on March 26, 2000, to consolidate his political power. In 2004 the Putin's government would use the "illegitimacy" of the acquisitions of wealth to go after some of the oligarchs who had acquired enormous economic and political power and who were controlling the media. Despite their vast accumulation of wealth and power, many of them were only in their thirties or forties. After 2004 the oligarchs would largely disappear from the news, except for those who had moved to London, while Putin's government would come under criticism in the Western press, particularly in the U.S., for going after some of these oligarchs and for nationalizing some previously privatized enterprises. As Boris Fedorov, a former minister of finance of Russia, would put it in a lecture given at the Carnegie Endowment for International Peace in Washington, Russia had created a "mal-functioning market economy" and the choice that it had was "a media controlled by oligarchs versus one controlled by the state." The oligarchs had made an active use of the media outlets that they controlled, following the classic golden rule that says that "those who have the gold make the rules." However, by 2007 the state had clearly won. The oligarchs had become politically more docile. Vladimir Putin, had succeeded in bringing them under control. Putin was named "Person of the Year" by *Time Magazine*, on December 31, 2007. As *Time* put it: [Putin] found a country on the verge of becoming a failed state. With dauntless persistence, a sharp vision of what Russia should become and a sense that he embodied the spirit of Mother Russia, Putin has put his country back on the map." Time continued: "Putin is not a boy scout. He is not a democrat in any way that the West would define it. He is not a paragon of free speech. He stands, above all, for stability . . ." (p. 45). Russia would become progressively more autocratic under the strong hand of Putin and his former KGB associates and, in part as the result of the commodity boom and the greater stability, it would experience several years of very high growth until the 2008–2009 crisis.

In the United States economists have stressed the importance, for economic development, of respecting property rights. Douglass North, an American economist, won the Nobel Prize in economics for emphasizing the importance for economic growth of institutions that protect property rights and that enforce contracts. Evidence from now-developed countries indicates that property rights are certainly one of the ingredients for a successful economy. However, the Chinese experience of very rapid growth in the last three decades, in a situation of uncertain property rights and questionable enforcement of contracts, has cast some doubts on this conclusion. Many individuals would feel uneasy about the state protecting property acquired illegitimately or illegally. It makes one think of a situation in which someone goes around robbing the neighborhood, or selling illegal drugs, and, once he has become rich from stealing or from drug smuggling, he campaigns for laws that will protect his property. It also makes one think about slavery in which existing property rights provided protection for the owners of slaves who had legally bought the slaves.

The important question is whether the protection of property rights can be separated from the legitimacy of the acquisition of the property. This is a very difficult question especially when what was legitimate in the past is no longer legitimate today. Anders Åslund, an expert on Russia and a coauthor of a recently published book on Russia, *The Russia Balance Sheet* written with Andrew Kuchins, has compared the Russian oligarchs with the American robber barons who built the American railroads and became enormously rich, getting free land from the U.S. government. By contrast the oligarchs got huge assets, often in natural resources, with the "loans for shares" programs. As Åslund put it: "the essence of successful capitalism is to accept existing property rights and declare them sacrosanct—*no matter how they arose in the first place*" (emphasis added). The justification for this is the Douglass North view that respect for property rights will "generate more economic growth." It may be considered populism but many will not agree with Anders Åslund. At the same time there must be a cut off point at which the past is forgotten and new clear rules are established for the future. It is not clear when that point should, or will, come for Russia. It is not likely to come soon, thus making it difficult to complete the transition to a functioning and mature market economy with democracy.

The Russian policymaker in charge of privatization was Anatoly Chubais. Chubais had been part of the group headed by Gaidar that in 1992 had talked about mass privatization. He was faced with a difficult problem. How could Russia privatize large enterprises, worth billions of dollars, in a country without rich people and without a developed financial market? In such a situation the only buyers could be foreigners, an option that must have seemed unattractive to him and to many Russians. An added difficulty was that many of the enterprises worth buying produced natural resources that, in a way, are God given. At that time the Russian government was under strong pressures from the World Bank, the U.S. government, the IMF, the financial market and many economists to privatize quickly. As mentioned earlier, privatization accompanied by the freeing of prices was assumed to be the quick road to a successful transition to a market economy. But privatization was not easy. Given the urgency and the outside pressures to privatize, as Chubais put it honestly in a 2004 *Financial Times* interview, the choice was "between bandit communism and bandit capitalism." He chose "bandit capitalism." He recognized that he would be remembered as "the person that sold Russia."

The process for privatization depended on "coupon privatization" and "loans for shares." Coupon privatization distributed shares in enterprises to citizens. At a time when incomes had collapsed, and enterprises were not making profits, these shares could be bought cheaply by those who had access to bank loans or to other financing sources, including foreign sources. Those who were able, somehow, to get financial resources to buy the shares (the coupons) acquired "property rights" over the assets and ended up with enormous wealth. This leaves open the question of how these individuals, often managers of the enterprises and well connected individuals, got the financial resources necessary to buy the shares in the absence of a developed, domestic financial market. Some got the resources from local banks that they themselves had established. Some from other sources. How much did foreign contacts or partners help? These individuals became the rich oligarchs who dominated the Russian scene during the Yeltsin years and who continue to hold huge amounts of Russian assets although their political power was reduced under Putin, and new actors entered the scene.

The "loans for shares" privatization gave capitalism a bad name in Russia. It created a feeling among the population that the Russian people had been cheated out of resources that were not even man-made but God-given, because they involved mostly natural resources. The oligarchs did not help themselves with their extravagant spending behavior that often made the news. However, they played a patriotic role by buying abroad, and bringing back to Russia, works of art and other historical items that reflected the Russian heritage, such as Fabergé's eggs bought at huge prices. Their intervention in the art market contributed to the increase in the prices of Russian art. At auctions Russian works of art often sold at many times the forecast prices.

Given this background, it is easy to understand why many Russians are not likely to appreciate and respect the concept of property rights and some of the rules necessary for the functioning of a market economy. Because economic power often creates political power, the establishment of a well functioning democracy was also affected. This is a mistake that the Chinese have so far avoided making, perhaps because the Chinese did not have large natural resources so that the wealth tended to be man made and could more easily be justified and attributed to hard work. The Chinese did not rush to privatize state-owned enterprises but let many new enterprises be created. The importance in the economy of state-owned enterprises has been declining gradually in China with the passing of time. However, other forms of corruption, often based on political connections, have been helping the well connected to become rich. This is creating a different form of resentment that over the long run may also create some difficulties in China.

During the mid years of the 1990s I went back to Moscow a few times mostly to discuss questions of technical assistance that the IMF was providing. I had some contacts with Mr. Barchuk who was for a while the Minister of Taxation and with Mr. Pochinok, whom I had met in Vienna in the early 1990s at the training center and who had become Chairman of the "Committee on Taxation, Prices and Plans" of the Supreme Soviet. During one of these visits, accompanied by some colleagues from the IMF, I visited Leningrad that had changed its name back to St. Petersburg. At the railroad station in St. Petersburg I noticed that the famous Lenin's statue had not been removed. The overnight train ride to St. Petersburg had been an interesting and not unpleasant experience. I had been happy to admire the splendor of St. Petersburg, the beautiful palaces, and the Hermitage Museum with its marvelous collection of French impressionist paintings that had been bought by aristocratic Russian families in the late 19th century and at the beginning of the 20th century. I was also able to take some stunning photos of St. Petersburg. One of these was a reflection in a pot of water on the ground of one of the churches. It was a marvelous, impressionistic reflection of the church.

The years in the mid 1990s were characterized by frustration about the deteriorating fiscal situation. Various attempts at reforming the relevant institutions had proved relatively unsuccessful. Superficial changes often hid the continuation of past habits or methods. At times I had the impression that only the package changed, not its content. I was reminded of a statement by J. K. Galbraith, in *The Affluent Society,* that the most difficult vested interests to deal with are those of the mind. Interests and mental habits, developed over 70 years, were difficult to change. Over these years corruption became a growing problem and concern. Regulations were often created mainly to extract bribes from the regulated, as Andrei Shleifer had shown in his book, *The Grabbing Hand.* Organized crime by Russians became a big concern not just in Russia but in some other countries where Russian "Mafiya" were reported to have become powerful. According to a French book in this period the different Mafias controlled at least 80 per cent of the Russian economy. See Renata Lesnik and Helene Blanc, *L'Empire de Toutes les Mafias.* In this period I remembered listening to some talks by FBI agents about the spread of Russian mafias in various parts of the world.

Chapter 4

Russia in the Late 1990s

In August 1999 I went back to Moscow to attend the Annual Congress of the International Institute of Public Finance (IIPF), the Congress that I had cancelled in August 1991 because of the attempted coup. I was no longer president of the IIPF so that my duties at the Congress were limited and I had time to enjoy the city of Moscow. During the recent years the IMF and my own department had been much involved with Russia. The IMF and Russia's agreement on a "Systemic Transformation Facility" had been agreed in March 1994; a "stand-by credit" had been agreed in April 1995; and in March 1996, the IMF had approved a three-year financial assistance program under the so-called "Extended Fund Facility." The Fiscal Affairs Department had continued to provide technical assistance to the tax administration and for the creation of a treasury office.

Things had not gone well in the Russian economy. In July 1998 there had been an "emergency program" that just a month later, had been followed by a kind of economic meltdown or default. The meltdown was the result of a classic "open-economy trilemma." This trilemma states that it is not possible for a country to maintain a fixed exchange rate when its capital account is formally or implicitly open, (meaning that money can easily come into the country or go out of it) and when its monetary policy is expansionary; that is too much money is being created, as was then the case in Russia. The meltdown had occurred only about a month after the international package of emergency financing, including a large loan by the Fund, had been announced. Thus, it was a major embarrassment for the IMF.

The aim of the financial package had been to maintain the exchange rate at its current level because of the belief, held at the time by several economists, including some within the IMF, that a stable exchange rate promotes fiscal discipline. This emergency package, pushed by Robert Rubin, then Secretary of the U.S. Treasury, and by Lawrence Summers, the Deputy Secretary, amounted to $22.6 billion, then a large sum. The meltdown had been a big embarrassment to the IMF but hardly a surprise to many Fund employees who could not understand what this program of financial loans could accomplish. When I went to Moscow in August 1999 there was still a lot of talk and newspapers' articles that discussed "who lost Russia." Some questioned how the Fund could have been so naïve in going into this agreement. Clearly a combination of political pressures on the Fund and wishful thinking on the part of some in the Fund's upper management had contributed to this debacle.

At this time newspapers' articles were full of stories about corruption in Russia at all levels. Money laundering on a large scale was also an issue. *The New York Times* was reporting that U.S. $10 billion had been laundered through a relatively small U.S. bank. As mentioned earlier, by 1999 a few Russians, the so-called oligarchs, had become enormously rich while the distribution of income within Russia, that ten years earlier had been quite even, had become very uneven, both among individuals and among regions. Those who controlled the enterprises were laundering this money. A technique called "tolling" was being used. This was an Enron-type technique that essentially used "transfer prices." Simply put, valuable materials (oil, nickel, etc.) were sold at low prices by a Russian company to a controlled foreign subsidiary. Subsequently the subsidiary resold the materials at the higher world prices. The difference became capital flight that needed to be laundered. Of course no taxes were paid on this money.

Corruption had become widespread and had reached way up in the government. The Yeltsin family was being mentioned with increasing frequency in connection with shady deals. This seems to be a common trait in corruption at the highest level. The families and the relatives of the leaders often take advantage of their positions as the "keepers of the gate," i.e., those who control access to the political leaders. Also in the news was the role that an offshore investment vehicle (FIMACO) might have played in channeling the money that the IMF had loaned to the Russian government out of the country or towards the Russian bond market. The IMF money was supposed to be kept in the reserves of the Central Bank, to allow it to sustain the level of the ruble. However, that level could not be maintained and the ruble was devalued on August 17, 1998. Some observers reached the conclusion that the Russians had lied to the IMF on the use of the loan and that the IMF had been taken for a ride. In either case this was not one of the glorious episodes in IMF history. The role played by some American investment banks in this episode was also being questioned. They had been encouraging clients to buy Russian bonds while the banks were pulling out their own money from these investments. This strategy on the part of the banks would be repeated on a large scale during the period before the 2008–2009 financial crisis. *The Washington Post* carried long articles dealing with this issue, and Paul Blustein, a reporter working at the *Post*, had written a fascinating book, *The Chastening*.

The Russian crisis of August 1998 contributed to the failure of Long Term Capital Management (LTCM), the famed Hedge Fund that had two winners of Nobel Prizes in economics on its staff—Robert Merton and Myron Scholes—and some of the presumably smartest guys on Wall Street. It turned out that this Hedge Fund provided much less hedge than its intellectually arrogant managers believed, or that the investors in LTCM had assumed. In some ways they had been fooled by systemic randomness, paraphrasing the title of a book, *Fooled by Randomness*, by Nassim Nicholas Taleb, 2004. In this case genius had really failed threatening almost the collapse of the international financial system and forcing the New York Federal Reserve Bank to intervene, presumably to save the financial system. A fascinating account of these developments can be found in Roger Lowenstein's book, *When Genius Failed*. The IMF was caught in the Russian crisis but just missed being caught in the crisis of LTCM. Its investment committee had wisely decided not to invest part of its pension fund in that Hedge Fund, in spite of some internal and high-level suggestions to that committee to do so. Some of the same developments that led to the failure of LTCM would reappear on a larger scale in the 2008–2009 financial crisis. In this case the Federal Reserve Bank would be unable to prevent a major crisis in spite of its intervention in the trillions of dollars justified, once again, by the argument that it was saving the system.

The 1999, 55th Congress of the International Institute of Public Finance (IIPF) was held at the Finance Academy, a powerful institution then headed by a formidable-looking Russian lady—big, blonde, matronly and with a permanent plastic smile—who seemed to be the poster of a Soviet *apparatchik*. She loved toasts and long speeches so that the participants were subjected to some of them, of course in Russian. The first official meeting was on a Sunday, on the 20th of August. It was supposed to be the customary Sunday afternoon working meeting of the Board of the IIPF, when various administrative details are discussed. The participants arrived just before 3 p.m., the time scheduled for the meeting. To everyone's surprise the Russian hosts had prepared a banquet with live music and an elaborate lunch. The problem was that most participants had already had lunch and this was supposed to be strictly a working meeting. Furthermore, that night, at 7:30 p.m., there would be the formal dinner for the Board members. Thus, the Board meeting had to be cut short and the participants had to talk, eat and listen to the live music at the same time.

It turned out to be a controversial meeting because of several sensitive issues: the need to raise dues for the IIPF membership; decisions on the publication of some of the papers presented at the Congress; and, especially, the election of a president to succeed the current one. Many Japanese public finance experts had become members of the IIPF for the first time in the previous few months and they had backed the nomination, for president, of Prof. Hiro Shibata a long-term IIPF member with a Ph.D. from Columbia University and author of several papers in good economic journals. He would be the first president of the IIPF from outside Europe or North America. There was some unhappiness with this development and especially with the large, recent increase of Japanese members, even though it was strictly legal and beneficial to the IIPF. This led to some sharp exchanges among the Board members. All this was happening while food was being served, the band was playing on, and the Russian lady kept smiling.

The IIPF members were staying at the hotel Aerostar, which had provided discounted rates for the rooms. It was a huge, Stalinist-era building in the middle of nowhere, far from the center of Moscow. My wife and I had decided to stay at the center of Moscow and had chosen the Metropol, where I had stayed in previous visits. It turned out to be a better choice even though the service seemed to have deteriorated further since my last visit. The ladies of the night, in the lobby and at each floor, had become more numerous and more aggressive. We were told that several of them were schoolteachers trying to increase their income to make ends meet! I tried to convince my wife that they were actually ladies who had forgotten their keys to the rooms and were waiting for their husbands to return! I had remarried in 1997 having lost my first wife to cancer in early 1995.

The theme of the IIPF meeting was the reform of public pension systems. The Minister of Finance of Russia opened the meeting. Yuri Lushkov, the charismatic mayor of Moscow, followed him as the second official speaker. The opening ceremony took place in Kolonny Hall near the Bolshoi Theatre. Kolonny Hall is an old, beautiful building that, before the Russian revolution, had been the club of the nobles. During communist times it had been used for formal occasions. The Mayor of Moscow gave what was essentially a campaign speech. At that time he was a candidate for the Presidency of Russia when, in 2000, Yeltsin would retire. However, he would remain mayor of Moscow and would win again the municipal elections with more than 90 percent of the votes. By the year 2010, his wife would be listed as one of the Russian billionaires. It was widely reported that Yeltsin and his family preferred to have a candidate that would protect them from likely prosecution for corruption. Their preferred candidate was Vladimir Putin, an ex KGB chief and an unknown until Yeltsin appointed him Prime Minister in August 1999. The "keepers of the gate" around Yeltsin were obviously worried about what could happen to them after the presidential change. The election of Putin in 2000 provided them with the needed insurance.

On Sunday morning my wife and I visited a very interesting outdoor market called Izmailovsky Market. Richard Highfield, a highly competent and effective resident expert on taxation from Australia, volunteered to accompany us. He was assisting the Russian tax administration on behalf of the IMF. While visiting the market, he gave me a detailed account about recent developments in tax administration. I was pleased to learn that things were finally going much better than in previous years and that, for the first time, the Russians were listening to the advice received and there were concrete signs of progress. At the market we bought a few things such as hats, Russian dolls, and old keys and locks for my collection. The keys and the locks were especially good and the prices relatively low. The Izmailovsky Market is very large and has a lot of interesting stuff. It is definitely worthy of a visit when in Moscow. There were many old icons but these could not be taken out of the country. They would be confiscated at customs on the way out, if discovered. For someone who wanted to take the risk, they could be good buys. I was told that one of our experts from Chile once bought one of these icons for $300 and sold it, in Santiago (Chile), a short time later for $3,000.

On Sunday night there was a dinner for the IIPF Board. It was held at the Metropol. Thus we were happy that we did not have to go out and, as usual, be forced to negotiate the price of the taxi fare. The taxi drivers often asked three times what they were willing to accept. Like almost everything else in Russia at that time, the taxi fare was negotiable. There were no rules or at least no rules that were enforced or observed.

The Moscow IIPF congress turned out to be a good one from an academic point of view. Interesting papers, on pension reforms, were given by professors Peter Diamond, from MIT, and Hans-Werner Sinn, from the University of Munich. I gave a paper, co-authored by Efraim Sadka, in which we showed that if large countries started saving and accumulating assets for funded future pensions, as it was being recommended, the rate of return on the accumulated assets was likely to fall, thus requiring higher savings than seemed necessary without taking account of this effect. Thus, accumulating assets to face future pension liabilities might be an easier policy for small countries but a more difficult one for large countries, especially if several of them chose this route. I also chaired a plenary session and a panel in which two theoretical papers were presented together with one that proposed a reform of the IMF. I was often amused by the *naïveté* of some of these academic papers.

The Finance Academy is a huge labyrinth where it took a long time to locate the room where a particular panel was being held. The instructions for the rooms were poor and I was reminded of the Russian cities in Stalinist times that did not have street names, presumably to make life more difficult for spies.

On Tuesday afternoon there was an excursion for all participants to an estate outside Moscow, Kolomenskoye, which had been the Tsars' village. It is a beautiful place with a small museum, filled with priceless icons, and with several beautiful, small churches. In one of these churches a fake wedding ceremony in the traditional Russian style was staged for the visitors. Professor Peter Sorensen from Denmark and his wife were married again! We enjoyed the elaborate and interesting ceremony. On Wednesday evening there was the banquet, a tradition for these congresses. It took place at the huge Moscow Hotel at the back of St. Basil's Cathedral. Each participant had paid $95 to attend but the food left much to be desired. However, there was entertainment and a lot of vodka and, where there is vodka, there are toasts.

I learned a beautiful toast attributed to a poet from Kazakhstan: "the past is history, the future is a mystery, the present is a gift." So, as the Romans would say: *carpe diem*; or, as the Russians would say, let us drink. I also learned about the rationale or the origin of toasts from those around our table. The Russian version was that toasts to good health (*santé* in French; *salud* in Spanish) originated at a time when it was not rare to poison your guests or be poisoned by your host. Poison was put in the drinks of those one wanted to get rid of. To prevent this, and to guarantee that the drinks were not poisoned, it became customary to exchange some of the content of the drinks, by pouring some of one's drink into the glasses of others and vice versa. Thus, if the drink had been poisoned, both would die. Perhaps, the expression, "to your good health" originated because of the chance of being poisoned by a drink that would take away your good health. Some colleagues from Northern Europe informed us about the origin of the exclamation "skull!" before drinking. Apparently the Vikings used to clean the skulls of their enemies in order to use them as convenient cups for their drinks. Calling for skulls meant calling for drinks. The Italians volunteered the origin of the expression "*cin cin*" used in Italy. They explained that, for Italians, a perfect drink should satisfy all the five senses. With some imagination it is possible to think that a drink satisfies the senses of touch, smell, taste and sight but this leaves unsatisfied the sense of hearing because drinks do not make sounds. So the *cin cin* (pronounced chin chin) is supposed to add the sound to satisfy the fifth sense. There were no Asians around the table to explain the origin of *kampai,* in Japan, *gunbai,* in Korea, and *kampei,* in China. I also learned about the great divide in Europe. It is not by nationality, or language, but by alcohol use. Just as Caesar's Gallia, Europe is divided into three parts: the part that drinks wine; the part that drinks beer; and the part that drinks vodka. It is an open question which of these parts is the happiest one.

During the five days we were in Moscow we went several times to Red Square to see if we could visit Lenin's tomb. But the lines were particularly long, perhaps because of rumors that Yeltsin would soon have the body of Lenin removed. Each time we marveled at the beauty of Red Square and of the Basilica of St. Basil.

The city of Moscow looked better than the last time I had seen it. Clearly the country and the city had started to recover from the economic downturn associated with the transition and from the default of 1998. It was cleaner and the people seemed less poor than in earlier years. There were fewer beggars in the streets, the streets were in better conditions, and the parks were better kept. A rumor was that Mayor Luzhkov had "invited" the beggars to leave town. Various good restaurants had opened and some signs of luxury had appeared.

With my wife we went to Arbat Street where I bought two nice naïf paintings by a Georgian painter. By this time the prices had gone up a great deal. We also visited the extraordinary Tretyakov Gallery. It was a real eye opener because of the beauty of the Russian paintings and icons that it contained. I had not known that Russia had produced such great painters and that icons could be so large and so beautiful. This was a real surprise and a pleasant experience. We enjoyed a great deal the visit to the Gallery although we had to do much walking.

We went back to Arbat Street and visited a large bookstore, supposedly the largest in Russia. We bought some calendars and art books. I realized that some prices were still distorted after almost a decade of transition. A beautiful art book had the same price as a cup of coffee. At least the subsidies were to art. We would also discover that a taxi ride to the airport was still equivalent to a month's salary of a schoolteacher. Clearly the economic transition had some way to go.

During this trip I visited Mr. Pochinok, who by now was the Minister of Taxation. He had chaired the Budget Commission at the Duma, the Russian Parliament, and had impressed me as a dynamic person who wanted to change things. I had met him at the Vienna seminar in 1992. I also visited Mrs. Nesterenko, the Treasurer. She was very interested in the hot topic of corruption and asked for some of the papers I had written on the subject. She requested that the Fund assist the Russian Treasury with training. The Soviet Union had not had a real treasury. Receiving and paying money, on behalf of the government, and keeping good accounts on these financial flow—the Treasury function—had been performed by a department in the Central Bank. It was a purely administrative function without any policy content. The Central Bank was expected to make any payment order it received from the planning office, by printing money when necessary. But a Central Bank in a market economy cannot continue to perform these functions so that the creation of a genuine Treasury had become necessary and a large amount of money (some U.S. $700 million loaned by the World Bank) had been allocated to this objective. This was one of the important institutional changes necessary for the transition from central planning to a market economy.

A well functioning Treasury, with genuine political power, reduces the financial independence of other institutions, including ministries, because the latter would need to channel their financial transactions through the Treasury, giving more power to the finance minister. Therefore, in the initial stage of the Treasury creation, some powerful ministries, such as defense, were allowed to remain out of the Treasury's control. Also, revenues directly raised by various public institutions, and not received from the government, would be left out of the treasury's control, as would the finances of the provinces and of various off-budget accounts. At that time many public institutions were leasing some of their buildings or space in them, selling some of their assets, and engaging in other commercial activities aimed at raising badly needed resources, in order to be able to continue to finance their activities and especially to pay their employees' salaries. This had become necessary because of the sharp cuts in payments that they were receiving from the government.

The system that was proposed by the IMF to the Russian Treasury was largely that of the Brazilian Treasury. It is a highly centralized and computerized system. The choice of this approach resulted from the fact that the IMF sent Brazilian experts—and mainly Pedro Parente, who later became a minister in the government of President Cardoso in Brazil—to advise the Russians. The Brazilian expert had recommended the Brazilian system that he knew well and that seemed to work well in Brazil. I had some doubts that it would work as well in Russia. This was a common problem in the provision of technical assistance. For some issues there were no *general* experts. All the expertise in some areas came from having worked on a particular issue in the country in which the experts had operated. Thus, there was a tendency to recommend to countries experiences that had worked well in one country but might not necessarily work as well under different circumstance. Unfortunately there was no good alternative. Academic experts were not helpful because even when they had a general knowledge of one area, they did not have the nuts and bolts knowledge necessary for this type of work. Their advice was often too general or too abstract to be useful in real life applications.

At the time of this visit corruption had become a common topic and examples of it abounded. For example, the police would routinely stop people in the streets to check if they had permits to visit Moscow. These permits were still necessary for Russians who did not reside permanently in Moscow. Liberty of travel within the country (and not just to go abroad) had not been part of the rights of Russian citizens. If the people who were stopped in the street did not have such permits (which had the same function as passports with visas for foreigners) a small payment to the police (a small bribe) settled the problem. This was one way for the police to round up their meager salaries. Fire inspectors and health inspectors would be very meticulous in their inspections to shops, restaurants, etc. to discover any small violation. Once again, when even minor violations of codes were found, the problem would be solved with a bribe, at least until the next inspection. Because of the low salaries that the policemen or the inspectors received, these small bribes seemed to be tolerated and they provided a strong incentive for careful inspections and hopefully for complying with regulations.

During our stay in Moscow, it was reported in the press that the airport immigration had been searching people leaving the country, to check that they were not taking out U.S. dollars. At that time Moscow seemed to be flooded with dollar bills helping explain the large amount of U.S. dollars in circulation. Various studies had shown that the dollar bills that Americans normally carried in their pockets and the dollars bills assumed to be in the hands of U.S. shops and banks were far below the estimated dollars in circulation. One explanation was that a large proportion of dollar bills were circulating abroad, many in former Soviet Union countries. In earlier years, when inflation was high in Latin American countries, a lot of U.S. dollars were in that part of the world. The airport searches made the participants to the IIPF meeting particularly nervous because many of them had brought dollars with them to pay for their stay in Moscow. We heard the story of a foreign diplomat who had imported a car by depositing $11,000 in a government account to be allowed to import the car. The deposit would be reimbursed when he left Russia bringing the car with him. This would prevent him from selling the car in Russia at a much higher price than he had paid for it. When he was ready to leave the country and asked for the return of his deposit, he discovered that there was no record of the $11,000 he had deposited. A payment of $100 to some employee made the record reappear. However, he got back his $11,000 in rubles, at the official exchange rate that had prevailed when he had made the deposit. Thus he got back almost nothing.

Given my interest in naïf art I wanted to visit the Municipal Museum of Naïf Art that I had seen mentioned in a tourist guide. Our driver took two hours to find the place. Nobody seemed to know where it was. People were not friendly to our guide who was a Russian-speaking Georgian who must have had a recognizable accent. When we finally found the place, it was two small rooms with very few paintings, a truly modest place. The two ladies who worked in the "museum" said that they received an average of one or two visitors a day. Hardly the Louvre!

In 1999 there were still unusual aspects or rules in Russia. For example husbands needed to provide a notarized authorization for their wives to drive a car or to use a portable phone. The tax police reported directly to the President on its findings. Bank checks almost did not exist. It was essentially a cash economy where many of the transactions were in U.S. dollars. One could get arrested for driving a dirty car. The Russian Treasurer received a salary that was only U.S. $250 per month.

Two days after we left Moscow, a bomb exploded at a shopping center near the Kremlin, not far from the Metropol, and many people were hurt.

Chapter 5

Putin's Russia

I went back to Moscow a couple more times after 1999. By that time this was Putin's Russia. The golden age of the oligarchs seemed to be over although many of them remained fabulously rich. Putin had won the election on March 26, 2000, and would win again on March 14, 2004. I went back to Russia in early April 2004, when I no longer worked at the IMF and I had left the Italian government where I had spent two years as an Undersecretary for Economy and Finance. I had been invited to participate in a conference on corruption to be held at the National Hotel, very close to the Kremlin, and to speak at the graduating ceremony of the Russian Graduate School of Economics. A Swedish Foundation covered the expenses of my trip. My wife, Maria, accompanied me and we stayed at a charming, small hotel called Hotel Budapest, a short walking distance from the Bolshoi Theatre.

The Conference took place a couple weeks after the election won by Putin. This timing might have made the programmed keynote speaker, the Russian head of an institution dealing with accountability in government, nervous to speak about corruption. A few days before the conference was to take place, he backed out. I was contacted and asked if I were willing to replace him in the program as the keynote speaker. I agreed to fill this more elevated spot. The conference was well attended and turned out to be very interesting. I gave a general lecture on factors that lead to corruption and on some of the economic consequences of corruption, drawing from several papers that I had written on the topic over the previous decade. My talk was not focused on Russia and, perhaps because of that, it was well received.

After my speech I enjoyed listening to other speakers. I noticed the contrasting views among them about the role and the extent of corruption in some of Russia's institutions. There was clearly no uniformity of views on the topic. This contrasted with the prevalent view abroad at that time and in later years. For example Åslund and Kuchins had come to the conclusion that "In Russia . . . corruption is the most serious popular concern." See *The Russia Balance Sheet*, 2009, p. 38. While some speakers argued that corruption was endemic in Russian schools, a participant stated that he had taught for 30 years in Russian schools and that in all that time he had never been approached by anyone for a favor in grading or in other decisions concerning students. He, and some others who spoke, believed that the talk about corruption in Russia was partly based on hearsay and was much exaggerated. It was repeated often enough to have acquired an echo and to have become a common belief.

Someone mentioned (as an example of the role that hearsay can play in countries) a story about Professor Albert Hirschman, the late development economist, in a visit to Mexico. Hirschman wanted to get the telephone number of a person that he knew in Mexico City but was told that, in Mexico, it was useless to call a telephone operator to get a number. Nobody did it because everybody believed that it was useless. A single, short call by Hirschman to a telephone operator had produced the phone number. Thus, there was a warning about accepting without proof conclusions that may be largely based on hearsay and may be exaggerated or just plain wrong. The speaker, rhetorically, asked how many of those present had experienced *directly* cases of corruption? There were few answers. He concluded that in Russia there was much less corruption than people believed. Other participants disputed that conclusion and argued that corruption was widespread and *was* a major problem. In any case the exchange made me think about surveys that produce indexes of corruption and that economists (including myself) have used somewhat uncritically in our empirical work. The responses must often be based on hearsay. Perhaps in the case of Russia an important distinction is that between "bureaucratic corruption" and "political corruption." There is widespread belief that political corruption is a major problem, regardless of the perception about bureaucratic corruption.

At the conference, there was some discussion as to whether various government agencies were doing enough to fight corruption. Some lamented that the agencies were not doing enough while others argued that the personnel of the agencies was itself too small or too corrupt so that it could not play the corruption reducing role. This led someone to comment that this was the same as complaining, after a meal in a restaurant, about bad food and small portions. If the food is bad, you do not want more of it. It was also pointed out that very low salaries were at times a strong incentive for acts of corruption on the part of some officials. Perhaps, the salaries were determined taking the corruption earnings into account. This conclusion, about the link between corruption and the level of wages, had been supported by some analytical work done at the IMF during my years there. It was pointed out that in 2004, the year of the conference, the *cash* salary of ministers in Russia was only U.S. $580 although ministers had various, non cash, fringe benefits. As some pointed out, the problem was that non-cash benefits do not buy some of the things that a person may need. For example they cannot buy school tuitions abroad for the ministers' children.

All in all, I found the debate more open than I had expected and generally of good quality. There was, however, no discussion of *political* corruption. The results of some surveys dealing with corruption in various sectors, such as education and health, were reported by some of the speakers. But the question remained as to whether wrong perceptions might not have biased these results. In any case, rightly or wrongly, Russia ranks among the most corrupt countries, according to Transparency International and other surveys, and its ranking has not improved in recent years. On the contrary it has got worse. In the 2009 survey by Transparency International, Russia's ranking among 180 countries was 146th with an index of 2.2 compared with a best index of 10.

At the graduation ceremony, at the "Russian Graduate School of Economics," that was held in a relatively modest building, some distance from the center of Moscow, I talked about the impact of globalization on tax systems. I got good questions and, in spite of the short interaction I had with them, I was impressed by the quality of the teaching staff and of the students. Many of the teachers had advanced degrees from top American universities and especially from MIT with which the school seemed to have a special relation. I was told that the students who graduate from the Graduate School were doing very well in the Russian job market that was improving at that time. At a dinner in the evening, in a nice Armenian restaurant, attended by some of the young faculty members, I learned about the strong mathematical orientation of many of the teaching staff, and especially about the reason for it. It was explained that during the time when the Society Union was in existence, many bright individuals chose mathematics because it was apolitical so that one had no constraints and no danger of becoming politically incorrect in a society where, for many decades, being politically incorrect carried dangerous consequences. Mathematics was a safe career choice. When the Soviet Union collapsed at the end of 1991, the mathematical skills of some individuals were channeled into economics. Some of these young faculty members came from places in Siberia. To my surprise they said that they preferred the Siberian climate to that of Moscow, because it is much drier so that the cold is felt less.

In the next few days, after my formal commitments were over, my wife and I set out to visit Moscow. The whether was splendid, clear and crisp, even though the temperature was still cold. We had made arrangements for a car and a guide to take us around. The guide, a colorful, lively lady with a slight limp, told us that, for many years, she had lived on the 15th floor of an apartment building in which the elevator was out of order most of the time. It must have helped her keep in good shape. She took us to see the "Park of Sculptures" where various sculptures from the past, some now politically embarrassing, had been taken, to remove them from more visible areas. At the park, we saw the statue of Dzerzhinsky, the founder of the Cheka (KGB), the Russian secret service. The statue had been removed from Lubyanka (or Dzerzhinsky) Square where the headquarters of the KGB was located. The Park had many other interesting sculptures including, especially, one dedicated to the victims of Stalin's persecutions. It consisted of stone heads placed behind barbed wires. After the visit to the Park of Sculptures we visited an exhibition of "totalitarian art." It contained official art from Stalin's time, in Russia, and Hitler's time, in Germany. They both showed smiling and healthy individuals that reflected the dream, or the utopia, of a perfect future in which the individual would disappear as an individual and become a docile, willing, and happy possession of the state. Because the aspirations of the people would coincide perfectly with those of the state, the individuals would feel free in their official prisons. I suppose that this could be defined as a version of individual freedom.

We also visited the "New Maiden Cemetery" near the splendid "New Maiden Monastery." The Monastery is a beautiful complex that had been reserved for nuns from noble families. The Cemetery is extraordinary mainly for the number of tombs of famous and easily recognizable individuals that it contains. Gorbachev's wife is buried here and we were told that, although she had been criticized in life, for being much more glamorous and visible than the wives of traditional Soviet leaders, she was attracting a growing number of visitors in her death. Lots of flowers had been placed at her tomb. Khrushchev's tomb is also in this cemetery as are those of many of Russia's famous writers, artists, inventors and political personalities. Interestingly, the cemetery is not as monumental as some cemeteries that I had seen. Thus, the concept of equality among individuals had been carried to the afterlife.

After the cemetery we visited the famous new Cathedral of the Russian Orthodox Church (Basilica of the Redeemer), the Church was rebuilt on the spot where the old cathedral, destroyed by Stalin, to build a year-round, open swimming pool, had been. The new church is stunning and contains very beautiful mosaics and paintings. In the evening we went to the Bolshoi where we saw a stunning performance of Don Quijote. It is difficult to see a more perfect performance of a famous ballet than one sees at the Bolshoi. We admired the six-tiered theatre. However, we paid much more for the tickets than I had in my earlier visit in 1991.

We were impressed by the changes that we saw in Moscow since 1999. The pick-up in economic growth, partly as the consequence of high commodity prices and increased political stability, was clearly having an impact. The Russian GDP had been growing at very high rates since 2000. Moscow had always been a beautiful city but now it was beautiful *and* more cheerful than in the past. By now, at least in the center of the city, the roads no longer had potholes; it was clean, and it had an abundance of nice restaurants and shops. There was also a lot of rebuilding. The Gums shopping arcade, that for someone coming from large Western cities had been somewhat depressing, had become an upper-scale, shopping center that had little to envy the best western shopping centers. The streets were now filled with cars and many of these were expensive foreign cars. Attitudes were also changing. I was amused by an explanation that I received as to how the streets had become clean. I was told that the Mayor of Moscow had started to apply "capitalist incentives" to street cleaning. He had started competitions among teams of street cleaners, accompanied by citizen's surveys that rated how clean the streets were. The team that was rated highest by the citizens was given money bonuses. These were not bankers' bonuses but they did create some incentives to perform better. Thus, the Mayor had made a full transition from communist to capitalist methods. Economic incentives for individuals had become politically acceptable while they had been against official policies during the communist years. Recently the mayor of Moscow was reported to want to apply the concept of bonuses to weather forecasters. The better the forecasts, the more the money they would receive.

The last day before we left Moscow, we satisfied a curiosity that we had. We decided to stand in line to see Lenin's tomb. It was something that I had wanted to do for a long time. As we stood in a long line, with our cameras in our hands, one of the guards came to me and told me that it was forbidden to go inside the Mausoleum with cameras. I asked him what I could do. With a straight face, and in relatively good English, he told me that I had two options: a 100 rubles option and a 200 rubles option. He explained that the 100 rubles option was to walk some distance away and deposit the camera, for the period of the visit, at a given official place paying a 100 rubles fee. The other option was simply to give him 200 rubles and we could take the camera along with us. When I asked him whether the other guards inside the mausoleum would object to my carrying the camera, he replied not to worry because he would take care of it. Thus, for convenience, I contributed to Russian (bureaucratic) corruption and to the earnings of the policemen by paying him the 200 rubles. We went inside the mausoleum with the forbidden cameras indecently exposed. I must say that I was somewhat amused and slightly embarrassed by the experience. My wife reminded me that I had written articles against corruption and about the responsibility of individuals not to encourage it.

In the Mausoleum we walked at the slow required speed along the obligatory path that goes around the tomb of Lenin and saw Lenin's body. The amount of lighting inside the Mausoleum was limited but we were surprised by how fresh Lenin's face looked. One had the impression that he was alive and was just sleeping. The body is not inside a liquid as I had thought that it would be. It is a mystery how it is kept so fresh-looking eight decades after Lenin's death. The thought occurred to me that I might be seeing a perfect wax copy of the original. Recently, a Russian told me that Lenin's body is finally deteriorating so that it may not last much longer.

I returned to Moscow in early April 2007 accompanied again by my wife. By this time Russia had had eight straight years of very high economic growth and of falling unemployment. It had joined the group of the BRIC, which included also Brazil, China and India. It was a group of emerging markets whose influence was bound to grow, both politically and economically, in the world. These four countries account for a large share of the land area of the Earth and for almost half of its population. Professor Evgeny Yasin, Academic Supervisor, State University–Higher School of Economics, had invited me to participate in a conference dealing with "Modernization of Economy and Public Development." It would take place in Moscow, at the World Trade Center, on April 3–5. The conference aimed to deal with the twin objectives of "modernization of the economy" and "modernization of society," recognizing that these are separate objectives that may not necessarily be promoted at the same time or at the same speed.

The conference program was an ambitious one and had high-level political and academic participation. The few participants from foreign countries were lodged in a hotel some distance from Moscow's World Trade Center. We had been instructed that a bus would come to pick us up on the morning of the first day of the conference. When the bus came I sat next to an American participant. We introduced ourselves and exchanged business cards. He mentioned that he was at the Princeton Institute for Advanced Studies where he had transferred from Harvard where he had been a Professor in the Economics Department. He specified that he dealt with theoretical economics. I was a bit surprised because his name did not ring a bell. He was not among the group of Harvard professors who were often in the news and with whom I had had contacts. He was very pleasant and I recall that we talked about a few people that we both knew. We were going to be in the same panel at the conference. I was, thus, very surprised, and much embarrassed for my own ignorance, when the following October Professor Eric S. Maskin was named as one of three winners of the 2007 Nobel Prize in economics. It drove home to me how specialized and fragmented economics has become so that one may be in the middle of it, be very active, and still not immediately recognize a future Nobel Prize winner. The 2007 Nobel Prize was given for "mechanism design theory," or the engineering side of economics. It explains how optimal allocation operates when conditions for it are not ideal. Given the objectives that policymakers want to achieve, how should the mechanism be designed to achieve those objectives when "the invisible hand" is not likely to generate the desired result spontaneously? The other co-winners of the 2007 prize were Leonid Hurwicz, whom I had once met at a conference in Korea and we had both contributed to the conference volume, and Roger Myerson. Both Maskin and Myerson have Ph.D.s in applied mathematics and not in economics from Harvard University. Hurwics had written the earliest paper on this area a few decades ago.

The World Trade Center is a huge building, somewhere in the middle of Moscow, that can accommodate thousands of people in the main conference hall. When I entered the building I had the impression that all of Moscow was in it. After registering I was escorted to my assigned seat and listened to the plenary meeting chaired by Professor Yasin. This first meeting was made up of high-level Russian political figures. It included A.D. Zhukov, Deputy chairman of the Government of the Russian Federation, G.O. Gref, Minister of Economic Development and Trade, A.L. Kudrin, Minister of Finance, A.A. Fursenko, Minister of Education and Science, and S.V. Stepushin, Chairman of the Accounting Chamber of the Russian Federation.

The debate soon turned into an issue that had become very important in Latin America at that time: what to do with the large trade and budgetary surpluses that were being generated by the high prices of oil and other export commodities. The Ministers of Economic Development and of Education and Science sharply attacked the Minister of Finance for not allocating larger budgetary amounts to their ministries, so that they could "promote growth." The criticism had a ring of familiarity. A few months earlier and a few months later I would participate in conferences at the Economic Commission for Latin America and the Caribbean (ECLAC) in Santiago (Chile) and would listen to the same arguments and the same complains for countries such as Chile, Peru and others. What surprised me was the sharpness of the exchange. Kudrin held its own in his argument for prudence. He pointed out that the economic climate might not remain always so benign. Perfect weather may be followed by perfect storms. For the past several years the economic weather had been particularly benign for Russia. Real GDP had grown at exceptionally high rates since 2000 and the general government had been running very large fiscal surpluses (8.3 and 6.8 percent of GDP in 2006 and 2007). The share of public debt into GDP was very low and large foreign reserves had been accumulated. This was a different Russia from that of the 1990s. Prudence would pay off a couple of years later when the financial and economic crisis arrived and, in 2009, the Russian GDP would fall sharply (by a projected 6.5 percent).

A.N. Shokhin, then President of the Russian Union of Industrialist and Entrepreneurs chaired the Round Table in which I participated. It included Professors Yasin and Maskin as well as representatives from various institutions, including the World Bank and Goldman Sachs. The theme of the Round Table was "Modernization of Economy and Society." Several speakers pointed out that a fast rate of growth, especially if it is a consequence of high commodity prices for an economy that exports commodities, is not necessarily an indication that the country is modernizing. Modernization has to do with improvement in basic institutions (political, fiscal, security, justice and so on). In Russia these institutions were modernizing at a slower pace than the economy was growing. Professor Maskin compared Russia with China using as an example a car manufacturer that controls completely the companies that supply it with needed inputs and one that lets the suppliers compete among them. More competition provides a better "mechanism design" and brings better results. In China he argued, there was more competition than in Russia.

In addition to participating in the Round Table at the conference the hosts had planned two other activities for me: to give a lecture on tax developments at the Academy of the Ministry of Finance, and to give a lecture (an "Honorary Report") on "Complexity and Systemic Failure" at the Higher School of Economics. The first of these had not been planned in advance but it was a last minute request. When I went to the Academy, a friendly crowd met me with flowers. The large room where the lecture was given was packed. I gave my improvised lecture on developments of tax systems and there were many questions related to the future development of the Russian tax system, the impact of globalization on it, and especially on whether flat-rate taxes are better than progressive taxes. Russia was the only major country that had introduced a flat-rate income tax and there had been claims that, as a result of this reform, tax revenue had increased and the economy had grown faster. While not criticizing the use of the flat-rate tax, using some analysis that had been made by an IMF study, I questioned the claim that the flat-rate tax had generated more tax revenue and had contributed to a faster rate of growth. I also reminded the audience that the income distribution in Russia was getting more uneven and that fiscal instruments (including progressive income taxes) might be useful in dealing with this trend.

The following day I was supposed to be picked up at a given time to be taken to the Higher School of Economics, which should not be confused with the Russian Graduate School of Economics where I had lectured in 2004. When, at the appointed time, nobody came to get me, I asked a taxi to take me to the School. The taxi took a lot of time to get to the School because of traffic congestion and charged me an astronomical price, 1,000 rubles. I later discovered that the School was just a short walking distance from the hotel so that I could have walked there in a few minutes. I realized that

(a) Moscow's roads were becoming progressively more crowded with cars, and (b) that one needed to negotiate in advance the cost of a taxi ride in order not be to cheated. However, to negotiate efficiently one has to know the distance of where he/she wanted to go. Thus, this asymmetry in the distribution of information can often give the taxi drivers an advantage.

At the Higher School of Economics I spoke on the role of complexity in the fall of the Soviet Union's economy along with the role of complexity in the market economy. In the Soviet Union, as the economy had gotten more complex, the planners had faced increasing difficulties in controlling it. I predicted that complexity would lead to a financial crisis and to other problems also in market economies, as it had in centrally planned economies. My prediction turned out to be a good forecast. The paper had been written in 2006 and was published (in a book in honor of Mario Nuti, an Italian economist who had specialized on centrally planned economies) in the middle of 2007, well before the financial crisis exploded. The audience was made up mostly of faculty members of the Higher School of Economics. There was a lively discussion at the end of my talk.

By 2007 Moscow had changed even more than in 2004 and looked as affluent as any Western capital. Eight years of very fast economic growth had had a great impact on the city. The shops were carrying the names of famous fashion houses and the cars in the streets had become more numerous and of better quality. There were many ethnic restaurants and the prices had gone sharply up. Some of the colossal buildings built during Stalin's time had been converted in very expensive condominiums. Moscow had become one of the most expensive cities in the world. My wife and I were invited to a famous Russian restaurant by the IMF resident representative and enjoyed typical Russian food. There was a lot of discussion at that time about the succession to Putin. At the restaurant our host explained to us that the concerns about democracy that were expressed in the Western Press were not echoed in Russia. For Russians, security and international prestige, that are characteristics of a strong country, were far more important. That is why Putin remained very popular. He was seen as the strong leader that many Russians felt Russia needed. Many Russians still see the fall of the Soviet Union as an act of betrayal and a national tragedy. That fall removed it from the status of a superpower.

During this visit I learned about a significant source of revenue for the city of Moscow. Because the municipality still owned all the land, all the new buildings had to rent it from the city by giving half of the new space created to the city government that could in turn rent the space and thus obtain non-tax revenue. This form of revenue-getting should be studied more by public finance experts. Similar sources of public revenue are also very important in China. They allow traditional taxes to remain low and may distort the official data on taxation.

On the last day in Moscow we decided to visit the Pushkin's museum that I had been told was very rich and worth visiting. There was a special exhibition of paintings by Modigliani that we enjoyed. We then visited the remarkable collection of French impressionist paintings. During the period of French impressionism noble Russians had bought many of the best impressionist paintings. Most of these are now in the Hermitage, in Saint Petersburg, and in the Pushkin's Museum, in Moscow. When we came out of the Museum, it was raining and there were no taxis in sight. Thus, we decided to go into the Basilica of the Redeemer and wait there for the rain to stop. The Basilica is just across the street from the museum. When we entered the Basilica we found it full of people. There was some ceremony going on. We soon realized that it was a mass and it was the Good Friday Mass, before Easter. The head of the Russian Orthodox Church was performing the elaborate ceremony. The mass lasted a long time, some two hours, and we remained all that time fascinated by the beautiful ceremony and by the very elaborate rituals.

That night, our last night in Moscow, we visited again Red Square. It had been decorated with thousands of blue lights that adorned it perfectly. It gave it a mystic look. I had never seen it so beautiful. We took some marvelous night photos.

After 2007 I did not go back to Russia. In 2008 two important events took place. First was the global economic crisis that hit Russia in a particularly powerful way because of its impact on commodity prices. Russian billionaires were hit particularly hard. Much of their fortune was tied to enterprises that exported commodities. The second was the election to President of Russia of Dmitry Medvedev, presumably a protégé of Vladimir Putin, who retained much power as Prime Minister. Putin is expected to run again for President in 2012. There have been increasing signs that Medvedev is more interested than Putin was to modernize Russia and some signs of friction between the two have appeared. Only time will tell whether Medvedev will help modernize Russia and whether Putin will return as President of Russia in 2012. For the time being, Russia appears more stable and with a slowly modernizing economy accompanied by some modernization in its political apparatus. In August 2010 Russia, and especially the area around Moscow, would experience the hottest summer in memory. The temperature would rise to 40 degrees and enormous fires would destroy huge forest areas. The smoke would cause health problems for the citizens of Moscow. It was a reminder that nature is still in charge. Hopefully it was not a reminder that, according to a Maya prophecy, 2012 would see the end of the world.

Chapter 6

Hungary: From Central Plan to the European Union

In the case of Hungary, I could more directly witness some of the changes that took place between the period of central planning and communist control and the period that followed it.

My first visit to Hungary took place in 1973. I went there to attend the conference of the International Association on Income and Wealth, an international economic association mainly concerned with questions of measurement of income changes and other national accounts statistics. At that time, I was a professor of economics at the American University in Washington. I was coming to Hungary from a trip to Pakistan and Iran where I had gone on a speaking tour financed by the U.S. State Department. It was the first time that I would visit a centrally-planned, communist country so I was eager to see my reaction. Because of difficult plane connections, I had flown to Belgrade on Aeroflot and had planned to go to Budapest by train. There was a cholera scare in Italy in that period so that passports were carefully checked when the train crossed into Hungary. My U.S. passport indicated that I had been in Italy recently so the inspector did not want me to proceed. After some discussion, in languages that were not understood by the other party, he gave up and let me go on.

When the train arrived in Budapest I asked someone, who looked like a policeman, for information on where I could change some money. The guy simply looked at me for a moment and moved on, without saying a word. I was left wondering what to do. After a while, I saw a sign that looked as if it might mean exchange. I went into a large room where there were two long lines of people. I figured that one had to go to the first line to get a receipt and then go to the second line to get the actual cash. I guessed that this was a way to create jobs; or perhaps, to better control the flow of money. The whole operation took a long time and I was both hungry and very tired. When I finally got my forints, I went to the restaurant in the station, sat down, and ordered a soup. The soup arrived, and I immediately saw that there was a fly in the soup. I had been hungry up to that moment but my hunger immediately disappeared.

I tried to get a taxi, to go from the central station to the local station where I was to take a train to go to Balatonfured, a small town by lake Balaton, where the conference would take place. I stood in line for a taxi and waited a long time. Finally I got a taxi that took me to the other station where I waited again for the train. I finally got to Balatonfured. In this whole operation I discovered one of the fundamental experiences in living in "workers' paradises" as planned economies were called: one spent a large part of one's life waiting in line. Perhaps, this taught people to be patient and to follow rules. At the arrival in Balatonfured, there were no taxis to go to the hotel and I did not know what to do. During this whole trip I was carrying a heavy suitcase that felt progressively heavier. Finally, the private sector came to my rescue. Someone stopped and in broken English asked if I needed transportation. I told him that I needed to go to the Hotel Christina. He offered to take me for a given price. I was happy with the offer even though the price was probably much higher than the official price for an official taxi, which was not available anyhow.

The Hotel Christina was right by the Lake Balaton. Balatonfured, is a tourist town. At that time, it was also the town where high level communist party officials retired. Because life expectancy in Hungary was low, this meant that the town was also a funeral town. Retirees did not survive long the joy, or the stress, of retirement. I saw more funeral homes in the two days that I was there than I had seen in a long time. I do not remember much about the conference, attended mostly by economists interested in national income statistics, but I do remember that the lake, which is very shallow, produces good fish that the conference participants enjoyed.

The second time I visited Hungary was a decade later, in 1984. By this time I had left my academic post and was working for the IMF as the Director of the Fiscal Affairs Department. I went there at the invitation of Mr. Peter Medgyessy, who was then the Deputy Minister of Finance of Hungary. He would become Minister of Finance in the mid-1990s, and, in 2002, Prime Minister. I had met Dr. Medgyessy during my years as a member of the Board of the International Institute of Public Finance. He was part of the small group of officials, or academics, from communist countries that regularly attended the annual congresses of the IIPF. The general view among IIPF participants was that those who attended from communist countries were the better connected politically. They were able to get access to the very difficult to get foreign exchange and to the permits needed to go abroad from their countries. A prevalent assumption was that these peoples were members of the

Russian KGB, or of equivalent security institutions in their countries. When Medgyessy became Prime Minister, in 2002, he admitted that he had worked for the KGB but maintained that he had done it to protect Hungarian interests.

By 1984, Hungary was giving some modest signs of independence from the Soviet Union and had become, through its experimentation in economic policy, a kind of pilot project for other planned economies, as was Yugoslavia under Tito. It was doing so very carefully remembering the experience of 1956 when the Russians had intervened to put down a rebellion. Slowly the Hungarian policymakers were, grudgingly, allowing some private economic activities to exist. To the credit of Mr. Medgyessy, he was beginning to try to reform the Hungarian tax system and to make the prices of goods sold more responsive to market forces. During this period my department at the IMF, the Fiscal Affairs Department, started helping Hungary in developing a tax system that would become more compatible with those of market economies. At this time Hungary was considering the introduction of a value added tax, a radical idea for a planned economy. Hungary would be the first among planned economies to introduce such a tax.

During this visit Mr. Medgyessy asked me to meet the politically powerful Deputy Prime Minister, Mr. Jozsef Marjai who had been Hungary's ambassador to Moscow. Accompanied by Dr. Medgyessy, I visited him in his splendid office. After the usual greetings, Mr. Marjai, asked my impressions of Hungary. I thought that I was being polite and not patronizing by mentioning that I appreciated the experiments in economic policy that Hungary was carrying out which, I mentioned, made it a kind of pilot project among planned economies. I added that I was also impressed by the fact that the country looked richer than I had expected. I added that the center of Budapest did not look much different from that of other European capitals. To my surprise, Mr. Marjai did not seem at all pleased with both of my comments. Rather forcefully, he responded that Hungary did not want to be a pilot project but wanted to live peacefully with its neighbors, that I understood to mean, the Russians. At that time there were still Russian troops stationed in Hungary. They kept a low profile but were ready to discourage any explicit manifestation of political independence. He also stressed that Hungary was a poor country and that the appearance of wealth in the center of Budapest was not a good indication of how poor the country really was. Of course he was right on this point.

This was my first official visit to a planned economy, apart from the brief unofficial trip to Hungary in 1973. I could, thus, form some fresh impressions. I became aware that only a very small part of the real income of workers, the income that determined their standards of living, consisted of the cash money that they received as wages. That part could be spent at their discretion, on the relatively limited items available in shops or on available cultural activities. All the shops were, of course, government owned. Much of the real income of workers was received in kind so that it was the government that made most of the decisions on what the workers' income was spent on and provided the basic safety net. Additionally, many of the goods that workers might want to buy with their little cash were often not available. Especially services were hardly available. As János Kornai, the prominent Hungarian economist, had put it, in some of his writings, this was an "economy of shortage." Shortage, or non-availability of many goods, was the norm. Individuals had to spend hours standing in line in front of shops to buy whatever was available; that often was not much. Thus time was a basic ingredient in the consumption function of individuals and not just money. Individual preferences in this environment counted little in determining what was produced; collective choices, or better the choices made by the planners played the major role.

I was especially surprised by the lack of individual initiative and by the embarrassment of individuals to acknowledge the few private activities that they were able, and allowed, to undertake. I recall a visit to a collective farm in which I met one of the workers. During the conversation, with the help of an interpreter, the worker mentioned that, in addition to his work at the collective farm, he was privately raising a few pigs on his own, in the small piece of land that he could use for his own discretionary activities. He explained that he got up at 4 o'clock each morning to take care of his pigs, before reporting for the regular work at the farm, that was his official job. As a consequence his workday was very long. I remarked, jokingly, that in this way he would become a capitalist. He was very embarrassed and even disturbed by my remark and forcefully objected to it. I realized that, perhaps, the sharpest difference between a market-oriented, capitalist country and a communist country with a planned economy is that in the former individual incentives are encouraged and stimulated while in the latter they are discouraged and often forbidden. Individuals with strong personal incentives were seen as antisocial elements that disturbed the harmony of the socialist society. Ideology or collective responsibility was expected to replace private incentives or, using a derogative word, greed. There was no place for greed or for "invisible hands" in these societies. The "hands" were quite visible. They were those of the communist party.

Incentives are almost always attached to the actions of individuals. It is difficult to transform them into collective incentives, especially on a sustained basis. Strong ideologies or even religious beliefs, or patriotism, may at times create and sustain collective incentives. The communist ideology had tried to replace the incentives of the individuals with those of the masses. But while individual incentives often survive the test of time, collective incentives generally do not. As soon as the revolutionary or patriotic fervor begins to abate, the collective incentives begin to disappear. This happened in these centrally planned societies and contributed to their fall.

There was a lot of concern among the officials that I met during this trip about the growth of some private sector activities especially in the service sector. It was feared that they could generate high incomes for some people and create income inequalities that would lead to social tension. These societies could not tolerate rich (or richer) individuals among them. These activities were generally referred to as "speculations" and the earnings of higher incomes, on the part of some individuals, were considered derived from speculative, and basically antisocial, activities unless the individuals were major athletes or artists. I was asked by the Hungarian officials how to discourage these activities through the tax system. It was curious for me that, while in the West we tried hard to limit the disincentive effects on private initiative of high marginal tax rates and of the tax system in general, here the government was interested in creating disincentives through the tax system that would inevitably reduce economic growth.

I also learned that there was no official unemployment in Hungary; or rather, that, the unemployed were not in the streets but were, presumably working, in the public enterprises. The public enterprises were required to hire all the available workers, regardless of whether they needed them or not. Thus, as the cynics would say, the workers pretended that they were working, and the enterprises pretended that they were paying them. Cash (or take-home) wages were very low but the most basic necessities were either free or very inexpensive. Workers received also various kinds of fringe benefits such as subsidized food, housing, education, paid vacation and so on. Incentives for both individuals and enterprises had been driven out of the system.

There was a joke, that I would also hear in Moscow, that captured the situation. It was stated that Adam and Eve had to be Hungarian because they had nothing to wear, had only an apple to eat but had been told that they were in paradise! It should be added that Hungary was better off than most other centrally planned economies.

At this time the president of the Central Bank was a colorful man, well known among central bankers, called Dr. Janos Fekete. I paid him a visit and we had an interesting conversation about Hungarian economic policy during which he told me a joke that I still remember. A high level Hungarian government official goes to Paris on an official trip and while there he decides to visit a place in Pigalle, the famous Parisian red light district, that had been recommended to him by an Hungarian colleague. He has a letter of introduction for the Madame who runs the place. After presenting the letter, the Madame calls an experienced girl in the house to accompany the official into a private room for their "rendezvous." They have been in the room just a couple minutes when the girl rushes out screaming, "No! No! No!" The Madame is embarrassed and immediately sends another more experienced girl to the room, but the scene repeats itself. When it happens a third time with the most experienced girl in the house, the Madame calls the girl and asks her what on earth the customer wants that merits such a reaction. The answer: he wanted to pay in forints! Forints were worthless outside of Hungary at that time, and this joke was an indirect way for Dr. Fekete to make that statement.

During this visit Dr. Otto Gado, a friendly individual who had been an active participant in the activities of the International Institute of Public Finance, took me to a beautiful concert. It included Tchaikovsky's violin concerto. He also took me to a museum where I recall particularly seeing a painting of an American woman wearing shorts and with rollers in her hair, a cigarette in her mouth, and carrying a basket packed with all kinds of groceries. The painting illustrated the view, promoted in these countries by communist propaganda, that material goods do not necessarily make for a civilized and cultured society. For that reason centrally planned economies were more focused on particular cultural activities including the promotion of naïf art. The governments of these countries often supported some innocent and, especially, apolitical, cultural activities.

At the request of the then Minister of Finance, Dr. Kupa, in 1991 I visited Hungary again accompanied by an IMF team that included Tony Pellecchio, from the Fund, and Professor Sijbren Cnossen, from the University of Rotterdam in the Netherlands, who at one time had been a Fund employee. We had come to design a new tax system, one that would be more attuned to a market economy. By this time, after the fall of the Berlin Wall and the dissolution of the Soviet Union, the process of transition to a market economy had started.

In this mission, particular issues that the minister wanted us to address were (a) the taxation of fringe benefits for workers, because such benefits continued to be important in the enterprises. Taxes that were limited only to cash wages would give little revenue; (b) the determination of appropriate depreciation periods for capital assets, to be used in the determination of the taxes on enterprise profits. The lives of assets used in centrally planned economies were much too long compared with those used in free market countries. The reason for using long lives had been that the central planners, and not the managers of the enterprises, would decide whether depreciation funds should be reinvested in the same activities; and (c) the elimination of some tax preferences that had no justifications in a market economy, as for example the preferential tax treatment accorded to the incomes of writers, artists, and athletes. These individuals did not receive wages from public enterprises, as most taxpayers did, and their earnings had been lightly taxed. If they had been successful in their activities, both in Hungary and abroad, these privileged taxpayers could receive high (and often foreign) incomes. For political reasons, these particular incomes had not been seen as incomes from "speculation" or from anti-social and individual efforts. Therefore, they had been taxed at very low rates also to prevent the emigration of these individuals.

During this mission I met with some members of Parliament who wanted to introduce flat-rate taxes, having accepted the supply-siders arguments in support of such taxes imposed, of course, with very low rates. The problem was that the level of public spending in Hungary was very high (above 45 percent of GDP) and there were no prospects of lowering it soon. Thus, Hungary would continue to need high tax revenue. This high public spending would continue to create fiscal problems for Hungary all the way to current days, when Hungary would need to go to the IMF for financial assistance. Supply-side economics does not tell us how to finance large public spending with low tax rates when that spending cannot be lowered. Some supply siders believe in the miracle of a Laffer curve in which lower tax rates magically provide higher revenue. Unfortunately, taxation is not an area where miracles happen, as many countries have discovered over the years. I recalled a luncheon, in the early 1980s, attended by Jack Kemp, the late football player, then a presidential candidate, who was one of the advocates of low taxes. During the luncheon, he had argued that developing countries should slash taxes and freeze exchange rates in order to become rich. That is all that they needed to do! There was no mention of public spending and of how reduce or to finance it. Presumably, the low taxes would finance, through the extreme version of the Laffer curve, whatever level of public spending.

At the end of the mission, following a tradition common to Fund missions, I decided to invite some of the people at the ministry of finance to a farewell dinner. They had helped us with the preparation of the technical assistance report that we would leave for the minister. The Fund mission included Mrs. Ana Maria Handford, from Uruguay, who had been responsible for typing the report and for making administrative arrangements. I asked Ana Maria to find a good but reasonably priced restaurant where we could have the dinner. We would be about ten people all together. She made some inquiries and came up with a name of what would be a good place to dine. I figured that because, at that time, a normal dinner in Budapest cost about $20 per person, a budget of $400, converted to forints, would be more than sufficient to pay for the dinner for the ten people.

We met at the restaurant which was in the basement of a building in the center of Budapest. Patrons had to go down some stairs from the street. When the guests arrived, we sat down and we were exactly ten. I asked the waiter for the menu but was told that there was no menu. He immediately mentioned that they had the best Russian caviar and the best French champagne. I tried to learn what good Hungarian food was available. At that point the waiter lost interest in me and approached our Hungarian guests offering them the most expensive items. Well, while we were being serenaded with violins, we spent the night consuming expensive Russian caviar and French champagne. I knew that we were being taken for a ride but there was nothing I could do because of the presence of our guests. When I got the bill, it was about four times the budget I had planned for. I did not have enough money with me to pay for it and, at that time, credit cards were not accepted. Thus, someone from the restaurant had to accompany me to the hotel where I could change dollars into forints (at the hotel rate!).

I was particularly upset and embarrassed by this experience because just a few days before my departure for Hungary I had stressed to the staff of the Fiscal Affairs Department the need to be parsimonious in this kind of entertainment. My action had been provoked by the claim of a member of the department who had spent, in a similar occasion, what I had considered an excessive amount of money. He had spent much less than what I was going to claim on my return to Washington!

The report that the mission prepared played some role in the modernization of the Hungarian tax system. The Fiscal Affairs Department would also be engaged over the following years in the establishment of a Treasury office and in other fiscal reforms in Hungary. In later years, a former FAD staff member, George Kopits, would become the chairman of the Hungarian Fiscal Council, a newly-established, independent watchdog agency.

After a couple of other brief visits to Hungary, to discuss various public finance issues with government officials, I returned to Budapest for almost three months in late 1997. By this time Hungary was well on its way to becoming a market economy. The IMF had a program that allowed long-term employees to take up to one year of sabbatical leave once during their Fund career. Given my position within the IMF, it would have been impossible for me to be away for a year from the Fund. In most years I was not even able to use the number of vacation days that the Fund authorized. When I left the IMF at the end of 2000, I lost a large number of accumulated days of annual leaves, leaves that I had not been able to take over the years. In 1997,however, two special circumstances made it possible and especially desirable for me to go to Budapest on a sabbatical visit of almost three months. I was invited to spend a research period with Collegium Budapest (or the Institute for Advanced Studies in Budapest), a multidisciplinary research institution modeled a bit on the Princeton Institute. The timing for this sabbatical leave was perfect because, at the end of September 1997, I was going to remarry. My first wife had died of cancer in early 1995. My new wife, Maria, was a Fund employee and she had accumulated enough vacation time to be able to accompany me.

Maria and I arrived in Budapest on October 1, 1997. We had married the day before. We spent the first night of our marriage on the plane to Budapest. Collegium staff met us at the airport and took us to the apartment assigned to us. It was a fairly comfortable one, and probably a very good one, by Hungarian standards. But modern it was not! The apartment was located on the Buda side of the river about 15 minutes' walk from the Hilton Hotel and the Church of St. Matthias, both at the center of Buda. The walk was a steep one so that we got our daily exercise going to Collegium Budapest in the morning and coming back to the apartment at night.

After checking in at the apartment, taking a shower, and changing we walked in the general direction of the institute. For a while we were lost and could not find it. But we eventually found it. It was just in front of the Church of St. Matthias and a few steps from the Hilton Hotel. This is probably the most attractive area of Budapest. We were taken for a tour of the Institute that occupies a quaint two hundred years old building that at one time had been Buda's City Hall. We were introduced to some of the people and found everyone very nice. We were looking forward to spending three months here, away from the pressures of Washington and in a setting where I would be able to think without feeling guilty that I was not doing something more concrete than thinking.

After the visit to the Collegium, we went for dinner in one of the many nearby restaurants. The food was average but it was accompanied by violin music, as it often was in Budapest. In fact music seemed to be everywhere. After dinner, we went to our first concert, at St. Matthias Church. It would be the first of many concerts we enjoyed in Budapest. The concert was a menu of Mozart, Vivaldi, Verdi, Purcell, and Schubert. It was magnificent but we had a hard time staying awake because we had not slept at all the night before.

The next day, I had my first full day at the Collegium and started meeting my colleagues. I talked to two Russians from Moscow, a sociologist-economist interested in labor markets, and an historian, interested in Chinese history. From them I learned a lot about what was going on in Russia. I also met an American from Arizona interested in "evolutionary biology." Everyone at the Institute was pleasant and friendly. Assar Lindbeck, a well-known Swedish economist, would also visit for a while. The weather, so far, was good even though it was a bit cold. We walked a few times through the area of the castle which includes the former royal palace and is now the site for several museums. George and Susan Kopits came to visit us from Vienna where George was spending some time at the Vienna Institute. Both have a Hungarian background. George was a colleague in the Fiscal Affairs Department. They took us for cake at a nice café and offered champagne for our wedding. In the evening we went to a restaurant where I had chicken paprika and goulash soup. A violinist played for us and invited us to buy a drink for him and the band. When I got the bill, 2000 florins had been added for the wine bottle for the musicians! We bought "foie gras" and a bottle of Tokay, the famous, sweet Hungarian wine that we would enjoy over the weekend. During our stay in Budapest we came to enjoy "foie gras" and Tokay. Hungary is a major producer of both.

On Saturday, we got up late, had breakfast, and decided to go to Pest to explore the other side of the river. We took the funicular, from the area of the royal palace, down to the bridge that crosses the river. We passed by the Intercontinental Hotel (formerly Hotel Forum) where I had stayed in 1991 and walked to the center of Budapest. It is a lively area full of shops, restaurants, coffeehouses and lots of music. There was music everywhere and one could not escape it. We had a late lunch at an Italian restaurant but the lunch included a non-Italian plate of goose liver. We had cappuccino at an outdoor café facing the river, walked through a market where we admired some of the famous Hungarian embroidery, bought a few CDs to listen to in the apartment, and started going back. We bought tickets for the 8:00 p.m. performance of the Danube Symphonic Orchestra and went back to the apartment. We noticed that the name of the regular occupant of our apartment, whose name was still on the door, was "Wildsec" and we baptized it as "wild sex."

In the evening we called a taxi to take us to the Concert Hall. The ride cost less than $2. The Concert Hall (Duna Palota) is small, sits about 250 people and is absolutely charming. It is baroque in style with beautiful carvings of angels and various decorations of flowers plated in gold. The acoustics is also very good. The orchestra, comprised of some 30 members, was led by a dynamic young maestro with a clear sense of humor. We read that in this famous concert hall, world-famous composers, such as Bartók, Kodály, Kálmán, and Dvořák, had performed. The orchestra played compositions by Berlioz, Bartók, Liszt, Brahms, Strauss and Monti. I had never heard of Monti but his music was enjoyable. The price of the ticket was about $15 dollars per person. I figured that in a richer country it would have been impossible to listen to 30 good performers entertain 250 spectators for two hours for $15 a piece. This is one area where the "Baumol's disease" may be a realistic description of likely developments. William Baumol, an American economist, argued in one of his papers, that activities that cannot benefit from productivity growth are likely to become relatively more expensive when a country's income rises. He used this theory to argue that public spending was bound to increase, as a share of GDP, over time because many public sector activities (education, health, etc.) do not benefit from productivity gains. As Hungary becomes richer, what will happen to the prices of these concerts? At the end of the concert we took a taxi. The theatre attendants hailed the taxi and walked us to it, and we paid $2.50 for the ride home. By the way, we soon discovered that the taxis that one called on the phone were very inexpensive; however, those one hailed in the street were very expensive. Obviously, the transition, with accompanied regulation, was still not completed in this sector.

On Sunday we woke up late and had brunch. I worked for a couple hours and then we went out. It was a splendid day, mild and sunny. We went back to the area of the castle and started exploring the many beautiful paths along the river with splendid views of the Danube. I took a few pictures but ran out of film. We decided to have lunch outside at a restaurant called Sissi, just in front of the Royal Palace. By coincidence the *Corriere delle Sera*, the Italian leading newspaper, of October 5 had an article on Sissi. She was Elisabeth of Austria, wife of Francis Joseph. She had had problems with her mother-in-law, the archduchess Sofia, and had died a tragic death, assassinated by the anarchist, Luigi Luccheni, on September 10, 1898, near Geneva. She was loved by the population of Trieste who in 1912 had a statue made in her honor. The article described her as an original and a nonconformist, and compared her to Princess Diana, who had died just a couple months before, in August 2007. Both princesses had died at about the same, young age under tragic circumstances. Interestingly, in recent years Sissi has become the name given to marijuana in some parts of Italy. It is now common to see graffiti on Italian walls that declare love for Sissi. I had thought that Sissi was a much-loved girl until I was told that the name referred to the drug.

In the evening we went to the Hungarian State Folk Budai Vigado. It was a series of folkloric dances, mostly Turkish inspired, with a lot of slapping on the boots and the thigh and a lot of thumbing on the wooden floor. The music was quite monotonous and the dances repetitive. I did not enjoy the show as much as I had the concert the night before.

The next Monday, all the fellows of the economics focus met to discuss the joint program of research. It was agreed that I would write a paper on corruption in the public finances of economies in transition. That paper would in time be published, make the list of the top 25 journal articles by file downloads (2002–09 it was number 6), and create difficulties for me vis-à-vis the Argentine government, as described in my book *Argentina: an Economic Chronicle* (2007).

We met with all the fellows of the Collegium in the office of the Rector. There were some interesting fellows including theoretical biologists, evolutionary biologists, specialists in linguistics, historians, sociologists, mathematicians, economists, etc. I loved the interdisciplinary environment and thought that it would be a fun place to be for the three months. Each member was introduced and reported briefly on past work. At the end of the meeting a glass of Tokay was offered and was identified as: the "King of wines and the wine of Kings." In the evening the members of the economic focus were invited by the Rector to a dinner at a nice and old (1885) restaurant called Muzeum Kávéház Étterem. I had grilled wild mushrooms and stuffed cabbage, both very tasty. The food was very good and at reasonable prices. I hoped that we would not add much weight during our stay in Budapest.

The next day, I had lunch with George Szapary, a former colleague at the IMF, and George Surany, then the governor of the National Bank of Hungary. They took me to a nice restaurant at the Intercontinental Hotel. We talked about Hungarian economic policy and especially about how difficult it was to complete the transition to a market economy. They commented that policies could be changed but to change the institutions and the mentality of people needed much more time. Lots of activities were still in the public sector that had remained very large thus requiring high levels of taxation and growing public debt. Because many people benefited directly from these activities, it was difficult to eliminate them. This problem would continue to create major fiscal difficulties after Hungary joined the European Union. We also discussed the possibility that Hungary's GDP may have been underestimated because new service-activities, that had not existed during central planning, were not being measured properly.

George Szapary told us that as a child he had lived with his family in a large house at the back of the Collegium. In 1945 the area where the house was located had become a huge battleground between the German and the Russian armies. He and his family and other inhabitants of the zone had spent weeks in the area's huge, natural caves. He said that when the fighting was over, and they finally came out of the caves, they emerged to a different world: much of what had been a beautiful neighborhood had become rubble. He had left Hungary in 1956, during the uprising against the communist government. That uprising was brutally crushed by the Russians, who remained in Hungary until the dissolution of the Soviet Union.

In the evening we went to an "Opera Night" at the Duna Palota. We arrived early and had a snack of caviar at a little restaurant inside the theater. Caviar was still very reasonable in price. While we were eating we saw a casually dressed young man who looked vaguely familiar. He was the conductor of the earlier concert and he was going to conduct the program that evening. I was surprised by how different and less imposing he looked than when we had seen him earlier. I, thus, came to appreciate the power of a uniform and of a position. In his book on *The Pleasure of Finding Things Out*, in a section called "Epaulettes and the Pope," Richard Feynman, the famous scientist, related that his father had once told him that uniforms make people bow. Give someone a nice uniform and you will create an image of authority in people's minds. I suppose that nice clothes have a somewhat similar effect. Perhaps that is why people pay so much for good clothes. Without his uniform, the guy in front of us was less imposing, less handsome, and much more normal looking than the (same) guy who had conducted the orchestra the night before. Thus, uniforms and good clothes are similar to publicity or to good packaging in their functions.

Unfortunately, a similar process seems to take place, in a different context, with ideas. Over the years, I have noticed that the weight that ideas carry often depends not so much on their intrinsic value but on the rank or the status of the person who advances the idea. There is no democratic process that values ideas and no efficient market that filters them. A stupid idea coming from someone of high rank, such as a president, or a CEO of an enterprise carries more weight than a good idea coming from persons of lower rank. What is worse, the subordinates of the person of high rank often make great efforts to prove that the idea advanced by their chief or superior has more depth or more value than it has. One could argue that the fact that someone has reached a high rank or a high position is a guarantee that his ideas will not be stupid. However, one runs into Carlo Cipolla's "fundamental laws of human stupidity." In a charming, little book in Italian called *Allegro ma non Troppo*, (Il Mulino: 1988), Cipolla, a prominent economic historian, advanced his four *fundamental laws of human stupidity*. I will summarize these four laws:

First law: we tend to underestimate the number of stupid individuals in circulation. In fact as Albert Einstein once put it: "only two things are infinite, the Universe and human stupidity, and I am not sure about the former."

Second law: the probability that a person is stupid is not correlated with any other characteristics of that person.

Third law: stupid persons often cause damage to others without bringing advantages to themselves. Thus they reduce the efficiency of the economy and the welfare of society. There is a negative sum outcome in what they do.

Fourth law: non stupid persons tend to underestimate how much damage stupid persons can cause.

It is especially the second law that is relevant here. Cipolla argues that any *large* group, regardless of the components of the group, contains the same *percentage* of stupid people as any other group. Education, intelligence, rank, political position, or other characteristics do not change this basic conclusion. Thus, stupid individuals will be found among college professors, CEOs, presidents of countries, winners of Nobel Prizes, and so on. And, of course, stupid individuals will advocate stupid ideas which, coming from the high ranking or well known individuals, will acquire a following or at times will be taken seriously. Thus social, political, or economic positions can play for ideas the same role as uniforms play for individuals. They make them look more important and better than they are objectively.

The opera concerts had a bass, a baritone, a tenor, and a soprano plus the 30 odd orchestra members. The theater was only half full and we had also paid only about $15 per person. So the ratio of performers to audience was very high, at least one performer for every 4–5 spectators. The program, all famous arias from Italian operas, was very good. The soprano had beautiful costumes and sang divinely. The performers could not have been paid much and clearly received much less than they would have been paid in New York, London, or Paris. This means that the value of what a person does depends on the per capita income of the country where the person operates, a reality not welcome by many.

The next weekend, my wife and I got up early, called a taxi, and went to the Ecseri Flea market. It was a more interesting market than those we had seen in most other Western cities. It was a combination of junk stores and good antique shops. We spent four hours and bought a couple of locks, two keys, a (fake) Gallé glass, an icon, and a primitive Transylvanian painting of Adam and Eve on glass. I came to enjoy these naïf, religious paintings on glass and bought several of them during our stay in Hungary. Their prices were still very low but would go up considerably in future years. I tried to buy a very old and unusual lock but the price was higher than I wanted to pay and the seller was not disposed to bargain. On the way back we took a street taxi and paid three times as much as we had paid going there. Clearly the law of one price, which often comes with competitive or well-regulated markets, had not reached the taxis of Budapest.

On Sunday, we went to Pest again. We had some pastry at the very nice pastry and coffee shop at the Forum Intercontinental Hotel, bought two CDs by Marta Sebestyen, the singer in the movie, *The English Patient,* and came back to the apartment. The weather had become gloomy, and we stayed in to watch the news on TV. Fausto Bertinotti, the head of the Italian Communist Party, had made the Prodi government collapse in Italy, and in Saragoza, Spain, a guy was stripped almost naked, but miraculously not hurt, by a bull in a ring! He tried hard to cover his private parts so as not to go "full monty" in front of thousands of spectators. He seemed to be more concerned about covering his private parts from the thousands of spectators than about protecting himself from the pointed horns of the bull. The bull seemed to have a sense of humor and got definitely the last laugh. The guy had to run naked out of the ring, probably with a red face because of the embarrassment!

The following week I had to go to Washington for an IMF Board meeting to discuss two papers, one on "fiscal transparency" and one on "fiscal rules." These two issues were getting progressively more attention because of developments within the European Union and the developing crisis in Southeast Asia. The meeting lasted several hours and was interesting. There was the usual split among Fund Board members: a natural three-way split, just like Europe with its drinking habits, or Ceasar's Gallia. Arabs and developing countries on one side; Australians, British and Americans on an other; and continental European directors forming a third group. I also met with members of the Fund's Senior Review Committee, the Committee that approves the promotions of candidates, to discuss proposals for the promotion of particular candidates. There were the usual comments on whether a "specialist" should be promoted to a B-3 level, which is a relatively high career rank in the Fund. I commented that the Fund was becoming a place for jacks-of-all-trades with limited depth. If one acquired some specialized knowledge, his/her career would be in danger! This was happening at a time when the Fund had been pulled into specific structural areas in which it had limited expertise, as in its work in transition economies and in Southeast Asia during the 1997–1998 crisis. In most cases, the so-called specialists, were individuals with Ph.D.s in economics from top universities. Their mistake, or presumed weakness, seemed to be that they had acquired some deep knowledge in particular areas, such as banking, public finances, or others. This knowledge presumably disqualified them from advancement.

After this week of meetings, I went back to Budapest. I traveled the night and had almost no sleep but I went to the Collegium in the morning and spent the day there. In the evening, my wife and I went to a Vivaldi concert at the Parliament Building, an extraordinarily beautiful building. The concert, which included Vivaldi's *Four Seasons* and *l'Estro Armonico*, lasted a bit over one hour but what a spectacular hour it was! The combination of Vivaldi with first rate performers and the incredibly beautiful rotunda of the Parliament buildings created one of the most charming environments I had experienced.

After the concert we caught a taxi and went to a restaurant, near our apartment in Buda, called "Arany Kaviar" or golden caviar. It was a small restaurant and we did not have reservations but, after a bit of hesitation, we were given a table. We wanted to celebrate my return to Budapest. We felt like splurging so that we ordered the special offer on the menu. It included the best Russian caviar served with ice-cold Russian vodka, followed by the best Hungarian fish from Lake Balaton, prepared with an excellent caviar sauce. We accompanied the whole meal with an excellent bottle of Hungarian white wine. We ended up having a truly spectacular dinner. The price was high by Hungarian standards, but still low by international standards.

The next day, I spent many hours writing a paper on "Globalization and Fiscal Decentralization" that I would be giving at a conference in Turin (Italy). In the evening we went to St. Matthias Church, near Buda Castle, to listen to Verdi's *Requiem*. The concert was dedicated to Rezso Lanto (1927–1977), the founder and leader of the Budapest Youth Choir. It was the 70th anniversary of his birth and the 20th anniversary of his death. The church was packed. We were lucky that we had bought tickets. At least 150 singers, musicians, and choir members performed the *Requiem*. This is perhaps

Verdi's most extraordinary piece of music. It is a deeply religious piece even though Verdi was not a friend of religion. Once again the combination of high-quality performers, extraordinary music, and a beautiful building created an unforgettable experience. The whole thing was most enjoyable and, again, very cheap! Economic growth would definitely be against these bargains and probably against these large performances. I am told that, today, these activities have become much more expensive in Budapest.

On Sunday, we woke up late, had an abundant breakfast and went out. It was a beautiful day. We walked and walked. I took pictures of the Pest side of the river and especially of the Parliament building. We stopped for cappuccino and "torte" at the coffee shop at the Forum Hotel and continued walking. We walked by the little outdoor market by the Pest side of the Danube. They had the usual wares: handmade embroidery, dolls, Russian products, and so on. The Russian influence was still much felt on these markets even though the Russian military were no longer in Hungary. We continued walking in the center of Budapest and to admire the beauty of its buildings. The fact that Budapest was physically almost the same as it had been a hundred years ago gave it a particular charm. There had been no new building in the center of the town since at least the 1920s and some of the buildings that had been destroyed by the war had been restored exactly as they had been. As in Warsaw, the communist governments had attempted to restore some of the original buildings.

We also observed the poor upkeep of many buildings, especially apartments buildings, that had not received the government's attention. Many of them were still showing the signs of the battles that had taken place in Budapest more than 50 years earlier. The holes left on walls by machine guns and cannon fire were visible in many buildings. I had a clear evidence of the importance of property rights and legal arrangements for shared properties. The owners of specific apartments did not feel that they owned the common areas of the buildings and felt no responsibility in keeping them in good conditions. The concept of condominium with shared property rights and duties had not yet been assimilated. Nobody had the responsibility to fix the common areas, such as the outside of buildings, entrances, common stairways etc. In some buildings no repairs had been made to these areas since before World War II. An additional complication was that in some cases the original owners had left the country, when the communists had taken over or after the 1956 Russian crackdown, so that the property rights of those occupying the buildings were uncertain. This was also a problem for other Eastern European countries.

My wife and I walked to the Magyar Nemzeti Múzeum and spent a couple hours in it. It is a rich museum that contains many important historical pieces. I bought copies of old keys and admired the original ones in the museum. At the time of closing we had seen only parts of it and felt that we had to go back for another visit. On the way back we stopped at a McDonald's and, for the first time since we arrived, had some fast food dinner. In the evening I read in an Italian newspaper that a Slow Food Association had been created in Italy and its members were having their first meeting. The goal of the Association would be to try to preserve traditional recipes which were disappearing because they required too much time to prepare. Many restaurants had pledged to keep some of these recipes on their menus. However the high prices for these recipes is likely to discourage the demand for them. Will economics or tradition win in this context? It remains to be seen. Gary Becker from the University of Chicago, and a Nobel Prize Winner in economics, would probably argue that economics would win. Is it all a question of prices? Of the value of time? Of cultures? How do different countries, say the U.S. and Italy, react to the increase in the value of time that comes with economic growth? I was reminded that I had published a paper, co-authored by Howell Zee, a colleague at the IMF, in a major economic journal arguing that the composition of what people consume is determined not only by income and by the prices of the goods that they buy but also by the time people spend to consume particular products or services compared with other goods or services. Thus time may not only influence the production of goods but also the consumption of them. As incomes grow and time becomes more valuable, we consume less of activities and products that require more time to consume and more of those that require less time. More McDonald's in our future?

Returning home one night, just beyond the Vienna gate, a small creature was slowly crossing the street. We were sure it was a rat. It was going to cross our path if it were not crushed first by a car. While we paused to let the little creature cross the road, a car stopped and a man got out and approached the little creature that by now, had reached the middle of the road. We could not figure out what the man intended to do. To our surprise, he picked the creature with his hands and deposited it on the sidewalk in front of us. We hesitated to proceed but then we realized that the creature was a small porcupine, an apparently endangered species. We appreciated the gesture of the kind man. It indicated that some things not bought in the market were still considered valuable.

I had been working hard on the paper for the fiscal federalism conference that was to be held in Turin at the end of October. When I finally finished it, I was not pleased with the final product but I had to send it. In the paper I argued that with globalization more and more public sector activities will be sent upward, toward international organization, or downward, toward sub-national governments and especially toward municipalities. The national governments would be the losers over the long run because their power would be reduced. In 2007 I was the keynote speaker at a conference on fiscal federalism in Berlin and had the opportunity to rewrite the paper in a way that satisfied me more. It was published as "The Future of Fiscal Federalism" in a good European journal. The paper reflected a different kind of transition toward more global and more local decision making.

At Colegium Budapest I listened to a lecture, by a British linguist, on the origin of languages. I learned that this is a hot subject among linguists. The lecturer mentioned various theories about the origin of languages and rejected all of them. He concluded that languages originated in connection with categorizations. People needed to formulate "categories" before they developed words that described them. All houses may be different in look but each belongs to a category that we recognize as house. Apparently computers are being used to develop models that allow the progressive formulation of categories. I had read some of Wittgenstein's views on the subject but I could not tell whether they were the same views as those exposed by the speaker.

Our life in Budapest continued to be pleasant and interesting. We went to a wine tasting and selling shop and bought some good Tokay wine. It is a sweet wine that is produced with grapes that ripen in late October when they acquire a high degree of sugar. We learned that Tokay comes in six grades (*puttonyos*). Grade 6 is the best. I also heard, on the Italian TV, that in 1997 Italy would have the best wine in a century. This was something to look forward to. Probably this was good compensation for the fall of the Italian Government.

The progressive transition to a market economy made the time in Budapest particularly interesting for an economist. I enjoyed the multidisciplinary environment of the Collegium and the cultural activities of Budapest. The weather got progressively colder and darker but not unbearably so. We continued to explore the city. We went several times to the Opera House (a truly splendid building) for operas (*Tosca, Traviata, Barbiere di Siviglia, Turandot*) and for ballet (Balanchine choreography). We went to various concerts and continued to be amazed by the quantity, the quality, and especially the low prices of these performances. These activities had been highly subsidized during the years of central planning and continued to be highly subsidized during the transition. We considered whether we should buy a small apartment that would allow us to come back to Budapest on a regular basis. We were told that one could buy small, modest apartments at low prices. But we never acted on this idea.

We met a friend of the Kopits, Vera, who invited us for dinner at her small but charming apartment that had a fairy tale view of the castle area especially at night. The view alone made it a valuable possession. At Vera's we met a prominent graphic artist (Jaanos Kass). He gave my wife Maria a small book with his main output and sketched a caricature of her on the front that made her very happy.

During our stay, Maria took Italian lessons from a Hungarian lady. The lady spoke very good Italian and came to our apartment for the lessons. The cost was about $5 per lesson (for more than one hour). Maria made fast progress and enjoyed her lessons. Unfortunately when we went to live in Rome a few years later, and she took lessons at the Dante Alighieri School, she was faced with the old-fashioned and typically Italian obsession with grammar. They made her so afraid of making any mistakes that her Italian suffered.

One night Vera invited us to a celebration of Jaanos Kass. When we arrived, the place was very crowded and there was some classical singing. There we met a charming couple: a retired Italian diplomat and his Hungarian wife. They invited us to their apartment for dinner. There was another couple—a Hungarian diplomat and his wife. These two couples had met in Tripoli, Libya, and spent much of the evening telling horror stories of life in Libya.

The night of the Kass celebration we had a dinner invitation to join a small group at "Gundel," the world-renowned restaurant. It was the first time we had gone to this restaurant and the place far exceeded our expectations. It was truly world class: a large, charming place with perfect service, very good food, and exceptionally good gypsy music. At our table there was a rather unusual collection of individuals. There was Jaanos Kass and a British graphic artist (apparently also quite well known), a book designer, a leading baritone, a woman cardiologist, who made a point to give us her card and tell us that she also owned an ambulance service, and a few others. I could not help think that in Washington such diversity of professional backgrounds would be difficult or impossible to bring together. Our complaint in Washington was that at most dinners or parties most of those present were either economists or lawyers. Somehow in Washington people mix with those with similar professions. They stick with their professional tribes! Perhaps this makes them more efficient in their work but creates more one-dimensional individuals who are unable or uninterested to talk about anything but their professional activities and, perhaps, politics, sports, or weather, the usual common denominators.

We talked to the baritone who was sitting in front of us. He explained that he had to spend several hours in the morning training his voice when he had to perform at night. Apparently the voice, just like the body, needs to be exercised. This was something that I did not know. I had always assumed that a good voice was just a gift from God that did not need any training. A few nights later we went to the opera and had front row seats. To our surprise he was one of the singers (in the *Barbiere di Siviglia*). He saw us from the stage, recognized us, and made a point of waving in a clear but not too obvious way.

One night George Szapary invited us to dinner. He is the former Fund staff member who had left Hungary in 1956. He later became Vice-President of the Central Bank of Hungary. Szapary comes from an old Hungarian family. Near the Collegium, in a little square that was just under my window, there is a statue of one of George's ancestors on horseback. The statue is in bronze and the years have created a dark, greenish patina on it. However, the testicles of the horse are kept very shiny because people believe that touching them, or better, caressing them, brings good luck. It is the same idea as spinning with one heel on the testicles of the toro in the famous gallery in Milan dedicated to the first Italian king. There is also a similar place in Beijing, at the Temple of Haven. At times, during the day I would look out of the window and see some girls, smiling in a slightly embarrassed way, caress the testicles of the horse of George's ancestor!

The other guests at Szapary's dinner included the later President of the Central Bank, George Surany, and another older couple, a prominent professor of whom I forget the name. We spent a lot of time discussing subsidies to the arts, and particularly to music.

These had been large during Communism and continued to be large during the Hungarian transition. Some countries, for example Ecuador, have laws that require that a percentage of the total cost of large buildings must be spent on artistic features. In Hungary, there were obviously substantial subsidies that allowed the large musical output that we were enjoying. The question we debated: should the state subsidize these activities in a marked economy? The subsidies are often justified on grounds of positive externalities connected with these activities. The problem is that the direct benefits often go mostly to the higher classes, who make greater use of these facilities, however, the taxes that support them are paid by everyone. The prices of the tickets often cover only a small part of the total costs of these activities. Are there genuine externalities that justify these subsidies? This has been a big issue in Italy in relation to government subsidies to La Scala and the Scarlatti orchestra in Naples. Economists often argue against these subsidies unless they can be justified by identifiable, significant externalities. Would a reduction in benefits eliminate these activities; or would it just reduce the salaries of the performers and possibly the quality of the performances? What if a country eliminated the subsidies while others continued to provide them and thus continued to be able to pay higher salaries to top performers? With the international opportunities created by globalization for top performers, they would move to the higher paying places. The discussion did not generate an agreement. It should be recognized that this has been the argument to justify huge bonuses to bankers.

We went several times to the two main outdoor markets in Budapest: Ecsery and Petofi Csarnok. I bought several keys (some from Roman times) and old locks. My collections were growing rapidly while my bank account was going down as rapidly. I also bought several other primitive, religious glass paintings from Transylvania. They are charming in their simplicity. I looked at Hungarian current, *naïf* art but somehow I never made the decision to buy any of the modern *naïf* paintings. They were not cheap. *Naïf* painting had been much supported by communist regimes because it reflected a vision of society that was close to the regimes' liking. I bought some Russian icons because, at that time, Budapest seemed to be a good place to buy them. I had been told that, before they left Hungary, the Russian soldiers, who had been stationed there, had sold many of them.

We met some representatives of Sotheby who were very active in Budapest at that time. They were not economists but confirmed my view that, especially in that transitional period, the art market was still very inefficient because families that were undergoing financial difficulties had works of art of which they had no clear knowledge of the current international value. This created a classic case of what economists call asymmetric information. In these situations those who have better information and money can exploit that knowledge to make significant economic gains. The economic difficulties that most of the transition economies were encountering in 1997 were contributing to the increase in the supply of antique or collectible goods coming into the market. Bad times force families to unload items that in better times they would rather keep. Works of art play the part of precautionary wealth.

My wife and I left Budapest just before Christmas 1997 to return to Washington and to our work at the IMF. It had been a very pleasant and rewarding experience. In many ways it had been the most pleasant experience in our lives. By the time we left, the transition towards a market economy was well on the way. However it was not yet complete. Some of the bad (or, in the view of some observers, good) habits acquired in the previous decades continued to exist. This included the large economic role of the state. Institutional changes that should have accompanied the policy changes were slow in coming. Some laws and especially those related to property and other acquired rights were still being debated.

In time Hungary would make enough reform and would attract enough foreign capital to join the European Union. However, it would continue to pay a price for not having been able to reduce the size of the public sector that still reflected the over expansion of the period of central planning. Very high taxes were not able to cover the inflated public expenses, creating large and possibly unsustainable fiscal deficits. Hungary became the first EU country to apply for a joint IMF-EU loan. In June 2010, Hungary would join Greece and some other EU countries in contributing to worries in the financial market about whether governments would be able to continue to meet their debt obligations. It also acquired a new and more conservative government.

Chapter 7

Croatia: From Central Planning and War to Peace

Croatia is one of the countries that, in the early 1990s, emerged from the break-up of Yugoslavia and that started on the transition to democracy and to a market economy. In 1995 the Croatian government decided to hold an international conference on the economic transition. The conference would take place in the beautiful city of Dubrovnik, on the Adriatic Sea. The conference was organized by the Central Bank of Croatia, and especially by its deputy governor, Marko Skreb, in collaboration with Mario Blejer, then an economist at the IMF. Several high-level fund employees were invited to participate in what the government of Croatia considered a politically important event.

In the period immediately before the conference there were major safety concerns in the region due to the war that had broken out in the area after the disintegration of Yugoslavia. Fighting was going on in nearby Sarajevo, between Bosnian Serbs and Muslims. There was heavy shelling of Sarajevo and acts of atrocities were being reported daily in the international news. A few days before the conference, Bosnian Serbs had taken as hostages some UN troops and had chained them to places that were likely to be bombed by NATO airplanes. Two days before the conference, an American military plane had been shot down over Bosnia. The UN was asking for the release of the hostages and NATO was threatening more bombing. In turn, the Serbs were threatening to attack tourists in Croatia if Croatia continued to allow NATO planes to fly over its territory. In short, it was a messy and dangerous situation.

Dubrovnik was just a few miles from the fighting. At the IMF there was a debate whether or not to allow its officials to attend the conference given the circumstances. The IMF hoped that the Croatian authorities would see the wisdom of canceling or at least of postponing the conference, or moving it to a safer place. On the Croatian side, the authorities were probably hoping that the invitees would decline to come so that the conference could be cancelled without embarrassment or loss of face. Or, possibly, they wanted the conference to go ahead to make the point that they still controlled the territory where Dubrovnik is located. When the time finally came, everyone showed up and the conference took place as planned.

I flew Swissair from Washington to Zurich and from Zurich to Zagreb. Other participants arrived at the Zagreb airport at about the same time. The staff of the Atlas Tourist Company was there to meet the participants who included a beautiful Croatian female economist who was working in Vienna at the Austrian Institute of Advanced Studies. Because we had a few hours of waiting in Zagreb, before flying to Dubrovnik, we were taken for a tour of the city and for lunch at a lovely, old hotel. We particularly marveled at the Mirogoy Cemetery with its most impressive and monumental tombs and mausoleums. I have always wondered at the resources that societies invest in honoring their deaths. Some of the most important monuments in the world are burial places including the Taj Mahal in India and the Pyramids in Egypt. Zagreb had been shelled a few days earlier but had suffered little damage. I wanted to take some photos of the city but the camera was not working and I was unsuccessful at having it repaired. Being a dilettante photographer, I found this situation rather frustrating. Eventually, I found out that it was not the camera that was misbehaving but its owner that was ignorant. A simple switch needed to be moved to make it work!

In the late afternoon, we flew to Dubrovnik and, after a relatively smooth landing, were taken, by way of a high mountain road that follows the sea, to the Hotel Argentina. Along the way to the hotel, we noticed many demolished houses along the route. Many of the houses that were not completely destroyed did not have a roof because, being high in the mountains, the shells that fell on the houses came from the sky thus lending on the roofs. The hotel was stunning but rundown. A Croat immigrant to Argentina, who had returned to Croatia in 1922, after making a fortune, had built it. It has been a common feature of immigrants that become very rich in foreign lands to return to their native countries and to build something that will impress their patriots. It seems that wealth becomes more valuable to its owners when it can be shown to people that they know and especially to those known when the new rich were poor. The location of Hotel Argentina is truly magnificent. Its terraces offer a fantastic view of the sea and, on the right, of the old town and of the port of Dubrovnik.

The hotel achieved great fame in the 1920s and 1930s when it attracted world famous personalities, including kings, famous actors and actresses, writers and other artists. I was given a nice room with a balcony overseeing the sea. From it I could enjoy my breakfast in the morning while admiring the splendid view. The hotel was empty except for the conference participants, even though it was June, or the high tourist season, and the current price of the room was only $20 per night. The tourists had disappeared because of the danger associated with the nearby fighting and the associated difficulties in getting to the city. Dubrovnik, or Ragusa in the Italian language, has often been described as the "Pearl of the Adriatic." It had been a major tourist destination for a long time. It is a town with a rich history that goes back about a thousand years. Over the centuries, it was much influenced by its relations with Venice but managed to keep its independence for much of the time. It is a truly stunning town because of its location and its architecture. In 1991 the town had seen a lot of fighting and many of its walls were still showing the signs of heavy shelling.

At the Conference there were several high-level Croatian policymakers responsible for economic matters. The Croatian participants included the Prime Minister, the Deputy Prime Minister, the Ministers of Finance and Economics, the Governor of the Central Bank and others. It was obvious that the Croatian government considered the conference very important. It was a way for Croatia to rejoin the western world after the many years spent in the socialist sphere and as part of Yugoslavia. The group of outside participants included some prominent economists including Robert Mundell, who would get the Nobel Prize in economics a few years later, and several others. Local newspapers and TV showed great interest in the conference.

Croatian television and some newspapers interviewed me. They wanted my opinion on the value added tax (VAT) that the government was planning to introduce as part of the transition. Some of the questions they asked me were: Should the tax have one or several rates? Should the tourist and other essential sectors be exempt from the tax? Should medicines, books, etc. be taxed? Why is a VAT better than the turnover tax, a multi-stage, cascading tax that it would replace? These were the same questions that had been raised in Russia and in Hungary. I took the purist's point of view: the best VAT is one with the broadest base and only one rate. This is at least the purest point of view from a tax practitioner, and not necessarily from a tax theorist, point of view. It is better than the turnover tax because it does not distort the relative prices of what people buy and makes its administration much simpler. Pressures for special treatment by some sectors should be resisted. If not, other sectors would make similar claims and it would be difficult for the government to resist these claims.

The economic policymakers were happy with my statement because they were trying hard to resist the pressures. When I went back to Croatia the next year, I was told that the tax had been introduced and would become effective on January 1, 1997. It had come out of the parliamentary debate fairly clean. I do not know what has happened to it after that time. I should perhaps add that a "clean VAT" goes against the instincts of policymakers and especially of those raised under central planning where interfering with the market was the norm.

The conference was lively and relatively practical. My first official task was to comment on a paper by Robert Mundell, on the fall in production and income that had supposedly taken place in transition economies in those years. At the time of the conference newspapers were full of stories about the collapse of production experienced by economies in transition. It had been reported that in some countries output had fallen by more than 50 percent, and in a few countries by as much as 80 percent, compared to pre-transition (planned economies) days. Professor Mundell believed that the fall in output was the biggest fall experienced by the economies of European countries since the days of the Black Plague in Europe in 1348–49. That plague killed at least one third of the European population and, in many ways changed economic relations, as described by Norman Cantor in his book *In the Wake of the Plague* or in a more recent book, by John Kelly, *The Great Mortality*. Some economic historians have argued that, by changing the ratio of usable land to population, the Black Plague led to an increase in labor productivity that initiated a process that made economic growth possible in later years.

Mundell's paper had been assigned to me for comments at 11 p.m. the night I arrived to Dubrovnik. I read it between 3:00 a.m. and 5:00 a.m. The previous night I had hardly slept because I had been on the plane crossing the Atlantic. In my comments I raised doubts about the estimated drop in output and about its significance, pointing out that those who prepared the statistics (a) had very low salaries, (b) had an interest in magnifying the fall in output, and (c) did not have the right technical skills to measure output during a period of high inflation and large changes in relative prices. Furthermore, (d) much of the drop was likely to have occurred in useless investment and in defense spending. I also questioned Mundell's assertion that high marginal tax rates had played the key role in this drop. Being the recognized godfather of supply-side economics, Mundell felt very strongly about the effect of taxes on economic activity. This view about the effect of taxes on output had been endorsed by the editorial page of the *Wall Street Journal* that had made almost a religion of its belief that low taxes have magical power in rejuvenating economies. In the *Journal's* view, low taxes are always the basic or most important ingredient for economic growth. The European Bank for Reconstruction and Development (EBRD) had reported effective marginal tax rates for some transition economies that exceeded 100 percent although the EBRD later had substantially revised these estimates. I argued that, when collection lags are long and inflation is very high, as it was at that time, real tax rates tend to be much lower than nominal tax rates. The reason is that by the time the taxes are paid the value of the payment has fallen because of the high inflation rate. Mundell seemed to be particularly annoyed by my comments, that questioned the role of taxes and, the following day, during a round table, returned to them reiterating his earlier position.

My second official duty was to participate in a round table covered by the Croatian TV. I detailed the advice that I would give to a prime minister on how to promote growth *after* stabilization was achieved. For a while stabilization and high inflation had been the main concerns of economic policy. However, soon stabilization would be achieved and growth would become more of a priority for governments. My remarks were much appreciated and I was later asked to develop them in an article that would be included as an "Afterward" to the book on the conference. Cambridge University Press published the book, which was edited by Mario Blejer and by Marko Skreb who was then the deputy governor of the Central Bank. Over the next few months he would become the Governor, after the current Governor retired for health reasons. The Deputy Prime Minister, Dr. Skrego, took many points down and the following year, when the second Dubrovnik conference took place, he told me that the points had played a role in some of the decisions made by the government. It is always a pleasant feeling to be told that one has some impact! A Croatian magazine, *Banka*, published a Croat language version of the "Afterward."

During the round table Professor Gur Ofer of the Hebrew University of Jerusalem, and husband of Dalia Ofer, a leading scholar on the Holocaust, referred to how the fascist government that had controlled Croatia before and during World War II, massacred the Jews. Apparently the first concentration camp (against the Serbs) was created by that government. Many Jews had been killed in Croatia so that Israel had not yet recognized Croatia. Ofer's comments were likely to have embarrassed the officials from the present government.

Mundell's strong defense of the "Laffer curve" made the round table interesting and lively. The "Laffer curve" refers to the view that, (within a range), lowering tax rates leads to higher, rather than lower, tax revenue, because the lower rates reduce tax avoidance and increase economic activity. That makes the rate reduction self-financing. In 2010 U.S. republican legislators have argued in favor of maintaining the tax cut introduced by President Bush several years ago that would expire. They have argued that low and lower tax rates do not contribute to fiscal deficits. Mundell strongly believed that high tax rates were reducing incentives and creating major difficulties for economies in transition. Evidence to the contrary (i.e., very low ratios of tax revenue to the countries' national income coupled with high fiscal deficits, because of the difficulty to cut public spending) did not change his view.

The Prime Minister closed the conference with a televised political speech in which he affirmed the need to resist pressures to raise real wages in order to maintain Croatia's competitiveness. He referred to the threat of strikes during the forthcoming visit of the Pope to Zagreb, to commemorate the city's 900 year anniversary. The Prime Minister threatened to resign if the unions' request for higher wages was accepted by Parliament.

That Friday night we had been invited to the Club Nautico for dinner. Some singers entertained us with songs, most of which were Italian. There was dancing, including by the Prime Minster with the beautiful Croatian lady I had met at the airport. There was also a good deal of drinking.

Saturday was a sightseeing day. First the participants walked through the old town of Dubrovnik. We were given a short lecture on the history of the city, its origin and its relationship with Venice and with the Turks. Dubrovnik succeeded in keeping its independence for many centuries until Napoleon occupied it, as he did with Venice. The lack of tourists, in a town that had been a preferred tourist destination, was striking.

The walk was followed by a boat ride that evidenced the splendid coast. I took a lot of pictures with my camera that now was behaving properly. We stopped at a charming fishing village where we had lunch with mostly grilled fish at a simple restaurant.

When we returned from the boat ride, some of us went for a two kilometer walk along the path built on top of the thick walls that surround the city of Dubrovnik. It is a very good way to get a feel for the town. From this walk one can see the spectacular sights of the city and appreciate the multicolored roofs. Without this walk, it would be impossible to fully appreciate the true beauty of Dubrovnik, with its old buildings, splendid churches, narrow streets, colorful roofs, high mountains surrounding it, and beautiful coastline. I was particularly fascinated by the roofs and by how similar the architecture was to that of Puglia, the region in Italy just across the Adriatic, where I was born. Later I discovered that in the late middle ages (the 13th and 14th centuries) the same architects had been operating on both sides of the Adriatic. This explained the similarities of the architectural styles.

We finished off the evening with a dinner on the terrace of the Hotel Argentina. A group of 30 young men and women entertained us with folkloric songs and dances. They wore beautiful native costumes. This entertainment brought home to me the extent of influence of Turkish culture on this part of the world. Both the customs and the dances bore a close relationship to those that one associates with Turkey. It reminded me of some of the folkloric dances I had seen in Budapest. Unfortunately my evening was clouded by a phone call I had made just before dinner in which I was informed that my mother (age 85) had fallen the night before and was in a hospital with a broken leg.

After dinner, I went to bed hoping to get a few hours of sleep before waking up at 5:00 a.m. when I would leave for the airport to catch the flight to Zagreb. A diehard group led by a lively Spanish economist from the EBRD, Ricardo Lago, was up until 2:00 a.m. singing mostly Spanish or Latin American songs, such as "La Cucaracha" and "Cielito Lindo." They succeeded in keeping me entertained and awake until that time.

The next morning we left for the airport happy that the threat of Serbian shelling of the city had not materialized and that the conference had passed without incidents. During the three days, we had become increasingly aware of the potential danger in the area. The fighting Serbs, who had tried to take over the city a couple years earlier, and had been pushed back after much fighting and much shelling of Dubrovnik and the area around it, were only about 15 kilometers from the city and 5 kilometers from the airport. They had the capacity to fire on both of these targets, if they wanted to. Because of the danger, all foreign airlines had stopped their flights into Dubrovnik and only the determination, or the stubbornness, of the Croatian government had kept the city open and the few flights by Croatian airline coming in. The pilots had to make long detours over the Adriatic to avoid routes too close to the coastline from which they would be subjected to potential shelling. From time to time the city was shelled and the airport was shelled more often. So we were happy when the plane was in the air and was aiming for the Adriatic.

Later that day, when I was at the Zagreb airport waiting for the flight to Zurich, I ran into the governor's assistant of the Central Bank of Croatia who had been at the conference and had left after the second day, along with Mario Nuti, an Italian economist, and Hernan Bucchi, the former Minister of Finance of Chile under Pinochet. He mentioned that the airport of Dubrovnik had been shelled the day before at the time their plane was ready to take off. They had had the scare of their life! Later I learned that the airport had also been shelled the day before my departure. In Dubrovnik we had not been informed about these developments. I was happy to board the Swiss Air flight from Zagreb to Zurich.

The following are some bits of trivial information.

Two brothers of the Minister of Finance had been killed in fighting the Serbs since the declaration of independence by Croatia. The minister, a lively fellow with a beautiful wife, was a remarkably cheerful person in view of these developments.

Many centuries ago, the tails of the Kuna (*ermellino*) had been used as money because of their use as scarves. Because of this, the new government of Croatia had called its money the Kuna. However, the Croatian Fascist Government during World War II had also called its money the Kuna. Thus, some ambassadors had boycotted the ceremony where the new money had been presented because they had assumed a connection between the present government and the previous fascist government.

In Zagreb I found out that a small painting by Carkovich, a naïf Croatian painter, sold for $15,000. At an auction at Sloan's, an auction house in Washington, I had given up at $800 for a painting by the same painter. A few days after the conference I saw a painting by Carkovich at an exhibition at the Vatican museum in Rome. Clearly he was considered an important painter. This convinced me of the great importance of information in the art market, a market that is far from being perfect. I have been an active participant in the lower end of this market and I have never regretted it. The contribution of Croatian painters to naïf art is very important and the "Croatian school" is one of the major schools in the world in this style of painting. Painters such as Josip Generalic, Ivan Generalic, Ivan Rubuzin, Mirko Virius, Ivan Lackovic Croata and others have become well known among collectors of naïf art.

I discovered that St. Vitus's Day (my name saint) is the most sacred day in the Serbian calendar. I had always thought that Vito was exclusively a southern Italian name. The name had become internationally known in connection with Don Vito Corleone of *Godfather* fame. Don Vito, the Cosa Nostra leader in Puzo's book, came from Sicily, one of two areas in Italy (along with Puglia) where Vito is a common name.

I also discovered that the men's neckties were first introduced in Croatia. The Italian name for a tie, cravatta, comes from Croatia. Probably they initially served as substitutes for napkins to wipe one's lips.

It took 20 hours to go by plane from Dubrovnik to Bari on the other side of the Adriatic—Dubrovnik-Zagreb-Zurich-Rome-Bari—a direct distance of no more than 150 miles. I felt that I could have swum in lesser time!

On August 2, 1995, about a month after the conference, fighting broke out again between Croatia and Serbia. Dubrovnik was shelled again. We were lucky to have gone to Dubrovnik during the lull between fighting!

In June 1996 (25–28) the Central Bank of Croatia organized the "Second Dubrovnik Conference on Transition Economies." The timing was a bit awkward for me because I had to go to Guatemala to commemorate the 50th Anniversary of the Guatemalan Central Bank. I would then fly to Washington where I would stay just a few hours, go to Paris where I had a commitment at the Organization for Economic Cooperation and Development (OECD), and, after 24 hours in Paris, go to Dubrovnik. I had become a true, global jet setter.

This time the situation was more peaceful, although the tourists had not yet returned and the city was still largely empty, except for the local population who had nowhere to go. Foreign airlines still refused to fly into Dubrovnik. Ron Brown's plane accident had taken place two month earlier, near Dubrovnik. He was at that time the U.S. Secretary of Commerce in the Clinton Administration. When I heard the news of his death, I remembered that a few weeks earlier I had been sitting not far from him in a domestic flight in the U.S.A. I could be in Dubrovnik for only two full days (three nights) so that I would miss the opening day and the excursion day at the end.

This time the landing in Dubrovnik had been much more difficult because of high wind. When I was met at the airport, I was told that a dinner was being held at that time at the Club Nautico. Therefore, I dropped the luggage at the hotel and went straight to the dinner. When I entered the room several friends and acquaintances greeted me. I definitely felt welcome. Someone joked that it was the "Tanzi effect" at work.

The dinner was very good (the best Adriatic fish). By the way those who live along the Adriatic coast insist that the Adriatic fish is the best in the world! I would show my bias if I expressed my view on this topic. I joined a table with Mario Blejer, Mario Nuti and others. There was much singing (again mostly Italian songs) and much drinking. Fortunately, there were no speeches.

The next morning I had a breakfast of fried eggs with ham, coffee, and bread on the terrace of the hotel. During my trips I always felt that being away from home justified committing culinary sins that I would not dare to commit at home. The view of the sea and of the old town of Dubrovnik was spectacular, especially with a perfectly blue and cloudless sky. Why is it that old buildings have so much charm? Is our mind conditioned to see them in a different light or are they objectively more charming than most new buildings? This is a question that I have often asked myself without being able to provide a convincing answer. The shift from natural products, such as stones, to man-made products, such as concrete or glass, seems to have made new building seem less natural and less attractive. A few small boats were fishing in the calm waters of the sea. It was a bit colder than it should have been at this time of the year. This year the war was not so present and the atmosphere was more relaxed. However, the conference participants were still the only guests at the hotel and, because of this, they continued to receive the full attention of the hotel staff.

I discussed Italian economic policy with Professor Mundell who spends a lot of time in Italy where he had bought and restored a large, old house in Tuscany. It had been a great investment for him. He believed that if Italy fixed the lira to the Deutch Mark (DM), at 1,000 to one and eliminated three zero from the Italian currency, the Italian public finance problem would be solved. The reason was that nominal interest rates would fall by about four percentage points, thus saving the country a lot of money on interest payments. As it turned out, when a few years later Italy joined the Euro Area and fixed the lira to the DM at close to 1,000 to one, nominal interest rates fell substantially and the public finances improved significantly. However, the public finance problem was *not* solved. That problem has continued to dominate the economic discussion in Italy to the present days. Mundell may have wanted to upstage the late Franco Modigliani, an economist born in Italy who had been teaching at MIT, who was also a Nobel Prize winner in economics. At about the time of the conference, Modigliani had wanted to achieve the same objective as Mundell's by forcing the Italian inflation rate down to zero. Its reduction would reduce nominal interest rates and the size of the conventionally measured fiscal deficit. It was not clear how this lowering of inflation could be achieved. Obviously the search for simple solutions to economic problems is an activity that economists, even the very best ones, do not wish to abandon.

The meeting was once again attended by the most senior Croat policymakers. I had occasions to speak with the Prime Minister, the Deputy Prime Ministers, the Ministers of Finance and of Economy and the Governor of the Central Bank. I was also invited to meet with members of parliament in Zagreb but because of my early departure, it could not be arranged.

The second night of the conference there was a dinner at the *Taberna Rustica*, once again with fish, wine, and music. An added attraction that night was Jacob Frenkel, a former Professor of Economics at the University of Chicago, former editor of the *Journal of Political Economy*, and a former colleague at the IMF where he had been Director of the Research Department. He was now the governor of the Central Bank of Israel, in Jerusalem. Jacob had come all the way from Israel to address the dinner crowd. He had arrived just before the dinner and would leave the next morning with the 6:45 a.m. flight to Zagreb. He was a famous world traveler as two jokes that circulated at the time about him indicated. The first joke asked what was the difference between Jacob and God. Answer: God was seen more often and spent more time in Jerusalem! Second joke: two planes are crossing the Atlantic in opposite directions and collide. Tragically and incredibly, Jacob was on both of them!

Jacob addressed the controversy on whether countries should have inflation targets (i.e., should determine the desired rate of inflation, announce it, and pursue the monetary policy necessary to achieve it); or whether, if they are small countries, they should fix the exchange rate most likely to the U.S. dollar, as Argentina and some other countries had done at that time. Mundell favored fixing the exchange rate. Frenkel argued for the inflation target. He also discussed the issue of who should bear the burden of dealing with banking crises, an issue that had become important in 1996 and that would return to be very important in later years and especially during the 2008–2009 financial crisis. He emphasized that banking crises must be dealt with without relaxing the country's macroeconomic program which meant without letting the fiscal deficit rise. Thus, this would require a lot of fiscal tightening. He also stressed that one could not be over cautious in giving credit to the point that no bank ever failed. He cited Bob Lucas, another economist who would soon get the Nobel Prize in economics, to the effect that if one never misses a plane, he is spending too much time at airports! In other words too much prudence may be as inefficient as too little prudence. I didn't like the analogy but it helped make Jacob's point. I came away from the speech with the feeling that Jacob had grown from an academic economist to a wise policymaker. In view of what happened to the value of the dollar in later years, it may not be a good policy for a country to tie its exchange rate to the dollar, as Argentina discovered in 2001–2002 when it was forced to default. Some now argue that Greece may have made the same mistake by tying its exchange rate to the euro. Inflation targeting gained in popularity with some economists. However, it has itself faced the problem that it may be associated with asset bubbles. In more recent years Jacob would reincarnate himself as a manager of

AIG, the American Insurance Group, that had been at the center of the 2008–2009 financial meltdown.

During this conference, with Mario Blejer and a couple other participants, we visited the Synagogue of Dubrovnik, a town where, in the past, there had been a significant Jewish community. The synagogue was a small, old house on a narrow street. The old rabbi told us that only twenty-seven mostly elderly Jews were left in Dubrovnik. He also told us an interesting story that seemed to upset him a great deal. Apparently, during the recent war with Serbia, the synagogue's Jewish treasure had been taken to New York for safekeeping. Now that the war was over the custodians in New York, who had been asked to guard the treasure, were refusing to return it to the Jewish community of Dubrovnik. They argued that the treasure was safer in New York and should remain there because, if it were returned, it might be lost once the 27 Jews of Dubrovnik died. This raised an interesting question in my mind. Do the property rights for this historical treasure belong to the Jewish community at large or to the specific, Jewish Community of Dubrovnik? I thought of this issue but was unable to decide which solutions was the right one. For sure the argument by the New York custodians is a challenge to individual rights (those of the Jews of Dubrovnik) that form the basis of much modern economics. If community rights are seen to prevail over individuals rights, much economics would need to be rewritten. In this I am considering the rights of the Jews of Dubrovnik as individual rights.

The same afternoon we visited the "Arboretum Irsteno." It is in a villa built in 1502 and occupied by a then very rich and famous man who had a wife who was legendary for her beauty. Torquato Tasso, the great 16th century Italian poet, dedicated sonnets to this woman and her husband dedicated to her the *Dialogo della Bellezza*, a treatise on beauty. She must have been truly beautiful. I could not help wondering why today there are no women who become legends because of their beauty, such as Nefertitis, Cleopatra, Helen of Troy, or others. Like much else, female beauty seems to have gone through a process of standardization. When one looks at beauty context, the participants look mostly the same, as if they had come out of an assembly line, or from the same mold. Perhaps, as there is a distribution of income, there may also be a distribution of beauty. Development may make this distribution more even. There are fewer ugly women but also fewer truly beautiful women. My impression is that there is more variance in the look of women in poor countries than in rich countries. In advanced countries one rarely sees the extraordinarily beautiful women than one occasionally sees in, say, Peru, or Colombia, or Venezuela, or India.

A beautiful renaissance play was enacted in the fountain of the villa with witches and enchanted princes. It was beautifully done. Thinking of the beautiful woman who had lived in this villa, I was reminded of what Einstein is supposedly to have said when asked to define relativity: "put your head in a stove for one minute and it will feel like an eternity. Spend an hour with a beautiful girl and it will feel like a minute. That is relativity!" Perhaps if Einstein had spent an hour with the beautiful woman who had lived in this villa, it would have felt like a few seconds.

In 1998 I went back a third time to Dubrovnik for what had become an annual June conference. By this time the tourists had started coming back and life had started to return to normal. The transition had made more progress. Somehow the place, though always beautiful and perhaps even more so now that it was being fixed up, did not seem as exciting as earlier. The lack of danger made it more common. Even the Conference seemed more routine. The discussion of big issues had been replaced by the presentation of more narrow and more technical papers. By that time the world was undergoing the experience of the financial crisis of South East Asia which in a way was a distraction from the issue of transition. Martin Wolf of *The Financial Times* was the dinner speaker. He criticized the IMF for requiring prudence in the fiscal policy of the affected countries. As a good Keynesian, he argued that more fiscal deficits were needed to pull the countries out of their crisis. As it turned out the countries of South East Asia recovered rather quickly without the burden of large public debts. This advice has been repeated in 2008–2009 during the global financial crisis and the public debts of several developed countries are going through the roof. We shall wait to see how good this advice will turn out to be this time around. As a firm believer in fiscal discipline and as a believer in the wisdom of Cicero's view, that the public finances should be kept under control, I have been worried by the recent growth in fiscal deficits and public debts.

Part Two

Other Passages

Portugal

Somalia

Lebanon

Morocco

Chapter 8

Portugal: Transition from Salazar

In 1969 the Salazar government, that had ruled Portugal for almost four decades, came to an end. During António de Oliveira Salazar's reign the Portuguese economy had been largely controlled from the top and had become a highly regulated one as was typical of economies of fascist or authoritarian regimes. State-owned public enterprises were common and economically important. When Salazar died the country started the transition to a true democracy with a more market-oriented economy that would eventually take it into the European Monetary Union. Salazar had been an unusual dictator. He had ruled Portugal with an iron fist for a long time but had maintained an austere lifestyle, choosing to live modestly. He had kept the country out of World War Two. The Salazar government was followed by a transitory government and in 1975 by a very leftist one headed by Colonel Othello. Thus, the country risked of going from a fascist economy into a centrally planned socialist economy.

The new government had immediately shown a great concern for the income distribution, that was believed to be very uneven, and for the impact of the tax system, that was believed to be regressive, on that distribution. The Fiscal Affairs Department of the IMF, that was headed at that time by Richard Goode, an American economist, was approached and asked to do a "tax incidence study" of the Portuguese tax system. On the basis of assumptions on where the real burden of various taxes falls, a "tax incidence study" attempts to estimate the burden of the tax system by income classes. In other words it attempts to show the taxes that families at different levels of income (at different deciles) pay. Such a study indicates whether a tax system is progressive, proportional or regressive. If the system is progressive, the tax burden rises (as a proportion of income) with the increase in the incomes of the families. If it is regressive, it means that poor families bear a higher burden (a higher share of their incomes) in taxes than richer families. In the 1960s and 1970s these tax incidence studies were popular and were made for many countries by Charles McLure and by other economists. For the United States a well-known study of this kind was made by Joseph Pechman, an economist at the Brookings Institution. At that time good tax systems were expected to be progressive. In more recent years these incidence studies went out of fashion, perhaps as an indication of reduced concern for equity and higher concern for economic growth; or, perhaps, because the assumptions that they made became more suspect.

I had joined the IMF as head of the Tax Policy Division a year earlier. To conduct this study for the Portuguese tax system I went to Lisbon, accompanied by Luc De Wulf, a Belgian colleague at the IMF. Luc De Wulf was a specialist on tax incidence studies and would be invaluable in helping with the many assumptions needed to be made to get the results and in getting and processing the statistical data needed. We went to Lisbon in January 1976, in the middle of what, in the international press and in the American newspapers, was described as political chaos. There was a common perception that a leftists-led revolution was taking place. Additionally, at that time Portugal was pulling out of Angola and many thousands of Portuguese nationals were returning from Africa adding to the country's unemployment and economic difficulties. These two factors combined would make any country a chaotic place and, perhaps, one too dangerous to visit.

Luc De Wulf and I left Washington with great apprehension. However, once we got to Lisbon we were struck by the contrast between what we had been reading in the international press, and the life in the streets and in the government offices in Lisbon. We saw no signs of revolution in the streets of Lisbon. In spite of the fact that in January Lisbon can be cold, wet and windy, there were large groups of people in the streets, many of them Portuguese who had just returned from Angola, debating the political situation and freezing in the cold to which they were not accustomed. We saw no fighting, and the mood seemed to be excited but almost festive. After decades of a rather dull, authoritarian regime, that had prevented the country from growing, this must have been a truly exciting time for many Portuguese. Change was definitely in the air. Reading newspapers one often forgets that demonstrations, riots, or even terrorist acts are usually local occurrences. One can be in a country or even in a city where these events take place and never see or hear anything about them. When the media circulate news reports that these happenings are taking place, it contributes to a generalized feeling of insecurity.

At that time, the Governor of the Central Bank of Portugal was Dr. Jose da Silva Lopez and the Director of Research at the Central Bank was Dr. Anibal Cavaco Silva. Both of them were serious professionals and good economists. Dr. Cavaco Silva, who had a Ph.D. in economics from the University of York, would become, first, Minister of Finance, then Prime Minister, and finally President of Portugal in 2006. At the time when Cavaco Silva had studied economics at York University, York was a center of excellence for the study of public finance and several individuals from various countries who were to distinguish themselves professionally and politically had studied there. With the help of various employees in the Central Bank, in the Ministry of Finance, and in the Statistical Office we made our estimations of tax incidence and wrote a report that was published by the Portuguese government. The Report received a lot of attention in the Portuguese press and by the authorities. Its title was "A Distribuicao da Carga Fiscal por Grupos de Rendimento em Portugal"—"The distribution of the tax burden by income groups." It was published, in 1977, in a book: *Conferencia Internacional sobre Economia Portuguesa.*

As one would have expected, our conclusion was that the current tax system did not help make the after tax distribution of income more even, or more equitable. The tax system had so many loopholes, or so-called "tax incentives," that it looked like Swiss cheese. Furthermore, and this was very important and unusual, the tax incentive rules and legislation, that were supposed to be the legal basis for giving tax incentives, were not published. This was an extreme case of asymmetric information. It made the tax system wildly non-transparent. The government officials that made the decisions on the incentives had all the knowledge about the laws and, especially, about the regulations. The taxpayers had almost none. As a general rule, when government officials have this monopoly on knowledge and a lot of discretion, they will use their positions to extract bribes. It was no surprise that corruption at that time was a major problem in Portugal.

In advanced countries, it is taken for granted that supposedly "official" information is always fully and readily available to any citizen that asks for it. In some countries, such as the USA there are even laws that require this. But this is often not the case. In many countries it is difficult to get access to information that should be readily available and widely distributed. Government officials are aware that information is power and they do their best to keep it for themselves. What's more, governments prefer to keep information that may be embarrassing out of the public domain. They discourage access to information in many ways. I recall a tax mission I once led to Sudan where we found out that, in the whole country, there was only one copy of the property tax law. It was obviously a much used copy which was not given out for consultation, or for copying. Once again the knowledge was only on one side and that was not the taxpayers' side.

Even though the ongoing leftist revolution, led by Colonel Othello, was not causing dead bodies to appear in the streets, it was having important effects on the psychology of the citizens and on the prices of the real assets that they owned. Asset prices always seem to overreact to these political events. Because of the fear that the country would become communist, the prices of apartments had collapsed. Apartments in Istoril and Cascais, the famous areas along the Atlantic coast called the Coast of Kings, because various former kings had residences there, could be bought for as little as U.S. $10,000. The prices of antiques, that other barometer of economic psychology, had also collapsed. I bought 12 old maps of the Napoleonic campaign in Spain, and a large old print of Giuseppe Garibaldi, the Italian hero of the Unification of Italy, for very little. In the early 1990s I would see the same phenomenon in the prices of antiques in the Eastern European countries that I visited during the early years of the so-called transition toward a market economy. Icons, old paperweights, and other antique objects could be bought for little. However, in this case the supply to the market increased, because of the poor economic conditions at a time when the demand for antiques, coming from abroad, was still limited.

Perhaps a specific, concrete episode gives a good picture of the prevailing psychology of the Portuguese citizens at that time. Miguel Beleza was a Portuguese economist who later became governor of the Central Bank of Portugal. In 1976, he was a relatively young man who had some financial savings. When he saw the ongoing political developments in Portugal, he thought that it would be wise to hedge his bets. He invested his savings in a Rolex watch convinced that, whatever happened, the Rolex would stay with him and keep its value. Some time later he moved to the University of Cambridge in England to complete his economic studies. While he was there his Rolex was stolen. By that time the "revolution" in Portugal was over! Thus, as is often the case, he had overreacted to the situation and had paid a high price for it.

Another aspect of the "revolution" that surprised me was its effect on pornography. The Salazar period had been one in which publications had been censored not only for their political digressions but also for their presumed immorality. There had been a puritanical tone to the Salazar years as there often is under authoritarian regimes. Within a few months from the end of the previous regime, the streets of Lisbon were full of the most obscene publications one can imagine. Additionally the movie houses were showing the hardest porn that could be produced. The publications were prominently displayed on sidewalks so that anyone passing by, including small children, could not miss seeing them. The movies seemed to be accessible to all. One could not escape this hard stuff. It was everywhere. There must have been a strong suppressed demand for pornographic materials; or, perhaps, this was simply an expression of the newly acquired freedom. I wondered whether these kinds of expression contribute to the nostalgia for the good old times that many individuals often feel in later years for previous repressive regimes.

During this trip I discovered Amalia Rodriguez, the great Portuguese singer of "*fado*" songs. She had been a legend in Portugal for a long time. Our Portuguese hosts were amused and surprised that I had not heard about this great singer. I discovered the charm of the *fado* the typically Portuguese "genre" of sad songs. These songs must have had their origin in the fact that, being a country of navigators, many Portuguese men would go away for long periods of time leaving behind their families or lovers. A significant percentage of them would not come back. These tragic circumstances called for sad songs. I could not help but think of the link between the *fado* and the tango. They both often reflect the sad side of life, although the *fado* songs are sadder. The tango was the musical expression of immigrants in Argentina and Uruguay who had left their families in distant lands and would not see them for a long time, if ever. *Fado* is older than tango. It is about two century old and it also originated from the brothels and the slums as the tango.

Unlike the word tango, the origin of which is uncertain, the word *fado* translates broadly as "destiny." However, there is no English word that comes close to conveying the full meaning of *fado*. *Fado* is destiny as seen by the poor and the desperate. Thus it is not just a random, unknown, or uncertain destiny but a sad destiny, one with a sad or tragic ending. The *fado* reflects the tragic side of life and the songs tell mostly the sad stories of the poor. Appropriately, the *fado* singers, who are often women, always wear black, the color associated with death. In a male dominated society, it was the women who were left behind when the men went away to earn a living in the dangerous waters of the North Atlantic or in distant lands. The words of these songs, which in some cases rise to the level of poetry, reflect the sadness of life as seen by these unfortunate souls.

One song asks whether this *fado*, this sad destiny, was the reason for being born and whether it was the reason for living this life. It continues saying that "they came and destroyed all the poetry that was inside me" and asks: "can I continue to live like this?" This question is repeated over and over with a lament that breaks one's heart. Another song tells about the end of love between the singer and her lover: "when I sing, I sing for you . . . .but you do not understand my song." Still another tells the story of a boy and a girl with different *fado*. It concludes that this was a very sad *fado* for both of them because in love it is better to have a common *fado*, even one with tragic ending, than a different one for each of the lovers. According to this song, Romeo and Juliet were lucky because they shared the same tragic *fado*.

There are actually two main schools of *fado* in Portugal, one in Lisbon and the other in Coimbra, a historical little town with an important university and university life. The Coimbra *fado* was sung by students and is generally less sad than the one in Lisbon. It has also a higher male participation among singers. There are several other variations such as *fado de saudade*, *fado menor do Porto*, *fado batido*, *fado alfacinha*, *fado flamenco* and others. Some of these variations come from the former Portuguese colonies (Cape Verde, Angola, Mozambique, Brazil, etc.).

Listening to the *fado* songs, in *fado* restaurants, the casas de fado, now frequented mostly by tourists in an area of Lisbon called Alfama, I could not help asking myself about the impact that economic development has on this kind of activity or art. I asked myself whether a higher per capita income would make the populations choose less sad songs and music. As the "economics of happiness," a recent branch of economics, has shown, a higher income brings lives with less pathos, less sadness, and less "fado." Thus, songs tend to lose their sadness because life becomes more pleasant. My impression is that globalization may help preserve the traditional songs because it brings tourists who provide a demand for the traditional arts. I could not fail to notice that in the *fado* places in Lisbon and in the tango places in Buenos Aires many of the customers are foreign tourists. Because of tourism, many performers of traditional art find it easier to make a living. But this means that these songs have gone from being the spontaneous expression of the poor to becoming the entertainment of the rich. They are preserved as entertainment and not as the genuine expression of the feelings and the sentiments of the populations that produced them. However, there is still value in this preservation and one should be grateful that they are preserved.

I returned to Portugal in January 1983 at a time when the country was contemplating joining the European Union. By that time Colonel Othello and his government were just a bad dream. Democratic institutions had returned and some progress toward an economy more dependent on the market had been made. The purpose of my visit was a conference on "Economic Policy in the Enlarged European Community." It was coordinated by Paulo Pitta e Cunha and Jorge Braga de Macedo, the first a professor of tax law at the University of Lisbon and the second a professor of economics also in Lisbon who, for a while, had been at Princeton University. Pitta e Cunha's father had been a minister. Braga de Macedo was the son of a professor of history who was well known in Portugal. He would become Minister of Finance and, later, Director of the Development Center of the OECD. The meeting was held at the Gulbenkian Foundation in Lisbon, a remarkable institution that deserves a few lines. The Foundation took its name from its founder, Calouste Gulbenkian.

Calouste Gulbenkian was an Armenian born in Istanbul and educated in England as an engineer. At the beginning of the twentieth century he played a major role in developing the petroleum industry in the Middle East. He made a large fortune on the commissions that he received as an intermediary on oil contracts becoming enormously rich. He collected very good art and assembled a large collection of paintings, ceramics, furniture and other works of art. In 1942 after the Germans occupied France where he had been living, he left to go to America. He stopped in Portugal on the way to America and never got beyond it. He fell in love with the country, which, at the time was still a peaceful place when much of the world was at war. His wealth was so large that it rivaled that of the Portuguese government. His wealth financed the Gulbenkian Foundation, the Gulbenkian Philharmonic, the Gulbenkian Choir, and some other institutions. The Gulbenkian Museum in Lisbon is beautiful and contains a lot of first rate, Middle Eastern art and much else. There is, of course, a Gulbenkian Avenue in Lisbon. It is difficult to think of any other individual who has had such a great impact on a country of adoption.

The conference was attended by many Portuguese who wanted to make up their minds on the benefits and the costs of joining the European Union. The speakers were mostly foreigners. They discussed issues such as regional income disparities, the European Union budget, the role of special interest groups, the "telemetric" (i.e., the internet) revolution, and fiscal harmonization within the Union. Reading these papers now, I am impressed by the fact that while the answers may have changed the problems and the question have remained the same. For example, the paper by Pentti Kouri, an economist from Finland, wrote that "there are few signs at this moment that point to a significant recovery...[in Europe]." "Virtually every industrialized country is in the middle of a fiscal crisis." "We have the threat...of protectionism that threatens the very fabric of multinational free trading system." My paper concluded that there had been little progress in coordinating direct taxes in Europe. Some of these statements could be made today.

A couple years later I went back to Portugal because of a conference organized by the External Relations Department of the IMF in collaboration with the Central Bank of Portugal. The Conference took place in a hotel, in Istoril, facing the Atlantic. The first night there was a huge storm and the wind and the ocean waves were making such loud noises that many participants could not sleep. It made me think of the Portuguese sailors that would spend months at sea in small boats in which it must have been difficult to get any sleep.

At the time of the conference, Portugal had a high public debt and a very large fiscal deficit mainly as the consequence of loss making public enterprises that, for political reasons, had been difficult to close. It needed to reform toward more sustainable fiscal accounts and a more efficient economy. It was clearly an economy still in need of a full, economic transition. This transition was different from that of centrally planned economies, but it was still a difficult one. For example a loss making shipbuilding enterprise that hired a lot of unionized workers needed to be closed or reformed.

An interesting paper by Teodora Cardoso, a Portuguese economist, gave the dimensions of the problem. This paper made it clear that there was a major structural problem in the economy of Portugal and in its fiscal accounts. This conclusion contrasted with the recommendation of the report of a mission of well-known economists from the Massachusetts Institute of Technology that had recommended a Keynesian, fiscal expansion as a solution to

Portugal's problems. These recommendations were often made by foreign academics that had little time to study the real problems of the countries they visited and thought that, policies that might work in the United States might work as well elsewhere. There was a tendency to confuse structural problems with problem of deficient aggregate demand. Or, alternatively, to believe that expanding aggregate demand would help solve structural problems. This attitude would become a major problem in some transition economies. It may also have been a problem during the 2008–2009 financial and economic crisis.

At that time a lot of academic attention was being devoted to the issue of clarity in the signals that came from governments. Economists had come to believe that it would improve economic performance if governments declared clearly what their goals were for the inflation rate, the interest rate, the fiscal deficit, etc, and to specify the policies that they intended to follow to achieve those goals. Academic economists had concluded that clear signals and good and steady policies produced the best economic results. This was an important change in economic thinking. I was asked to give a speech at the official luncheon and tried to make the point with a joke. Reagan, Brezhnev and Mitterand, three important world leaders at that time, met at a summit. At the end of the summit each leader got in his official limousine to go to the respective destination. The limousines had to follow the driveway in front of the hotel and then had to turn right or left on the main road. Reagan was the first to leave. When his limousine reached the end of the driveway, the driver asked him which way he should turn, Reagan answered: right, always right! When Brezhnev got in his car and was asked the same question, he answered: left, always left! It was then the turn of Mitterand. When, at the end of the driveway, he was asked the same question, he told the driver to put the signal to the left and turn right! I concluded that I would not like to be a minister under Mitterand's direction.

At the Conference I presented a paper—written jointly with Mario Blejer who would later become President of the Argentine's Central Bank during a turbulent time—on "Fiscal Policy in an Economy with High Debt and High Inflation." The discussant of the paper was Dr. Cavaco Silva whom I had met in 1976, when he was Director of Research at the Central Bank of Portugal. After the conference he invited me for dinner at his, surprisingly modest, apartment. His charming wife, Maria, had prepared a dish of *bacalhau*, or dried and salted cod fish.

Codfish (*bacalhau)* has been very important in Portugal over many centuries. It was so important for the country that a fisherman who fished it for four consecutive seasons would be exempted from military service and from participating in wars. Cod fishing was a dangerous activity. Fishermen, some of whom could not even swim, went to the North Atlantic near Iceland, where violent storms are frequent, on small boats. Some of these boats would sink during storms. The fact that at that time Portugal had the best deposits of salt in Europe gave it a comparative advantage because the cod that was caught could be preserved in salt. The salted cod became a major staple for the Portuguese. In recent years Portugal lost its fishing rights in some of the best fishing areas of the North Atlantic so that the cost of *bacalhau* skyrocketed. This became a significant problem for the country. *Bacalhau* remains very important in Portuguese cuisine. It is served everywhere and, together with dried legumes, forms the basis of Portuguese cuisine. Cod fish has the lowest percentage of fat and the highest percentage of protein among all fish. Thus, it is a very nutritious and healthy food. A recent book by Mark Kurlansky called *Cod* has told the story of the "fish that changed the world."

I have often thought that the quality of the cuisine of a country is a very important element in the country's standard of living or quality of life. Economists have paid a lot of attention to per capita income and to the number of calories that people consume. But there are calories and calories. It must make a lot of difference to the quality of life to consume 2500 tasteless calories or 2500 healthy calories that reflect time-tested and delicious dishes. Perhaps standards of living indexes should be adjusted to include a qualitative index that reflects the average quality of a country's cuisine. Now that economists are developing qualitative data for many variables (corruption, red tape, civil liberty and so on) they could develop one for the quality of the cuisines. Ten would be the best, zero the worst. I would have ready proposals for many countries for these scores.

This leads me to an important question. Why do some nations produce great cuisines while others produce tasteless dishes? Why, for example, the British never developed an indigenous cuisine comparable to that of the French or the Italians? This must remain one of history's great mysteries. Explanations based on religious beliefs, that presumably made it a sin to enjoy too much one's food, are not very convincing. One of my Harvard professors, Professor Houthakker, who was Dutch, used to argue that, given the relative prices of basic ingredients, he could explain any traditional cuisine. But the story must be more complex than that. Even if he could explain the use of the main ingredients, he could not explain the quality of the final product. It is the quality of the output that is important.

How will the growth of per capita income and globalization affect the quality of the food that people eat every day? On one hand, globalization widens the range of ingredients available and the knowledge of other cuisines. On the other hand, the value of time rises, making it more costly to spend much time cooking or even eating. Perhaps we will end up with two categories of foods. Fast food for the masses. Refined recipes for the rich who can have servants cook for them or can patronize expensive restaurants. However, time has more value for the rich. Thus, the good meals will be reserved for special occasions.

Chapter 9

Portugal: Rejoining Europe

In 1993 Cavaco Silva, who had become the prime minister of Portugal, invited me to participate in a meeting organized by the Academia Internacional Libertade e Desenvolvimento. By 1993 Lisbon had changed dramatically since my first visit in 1976. It was much more affluent, cosmopolitan, orderly and clean. The bargain antiques had disappeared and the prices of apartments had skyrocketed. Two shops that I visited had Sotheby catalogues readily available and what they sold was too expensive to induce one to buy anything. The market had definitely become much more "efficient," in the sense that economists attribute to the term, and prices now broadly reflected international prices.

The orderly lines that spontaneously formed at bus stops or at the cashiers' counters in shops made a strong impression on me. I could not help comparing this attitude with those in Italy where at times there was less sense of order and less obeying of rules, especially in shops at peak times. I recalled an experience in Milan, at Linate airport, where I had waited in a long line for a taxi. A guy of about 40 years of age walked close to the front of the line and stood there, next to it, for a while, as if undecided on where to go or what to do. At a certain moment, when he thought that everyone was distracted, he simply cut into the line almost in front. When someone protested, he touched his leg and with a straight face said that he had a bad leg. I wondered if he would use the excuse of the "bad" leg to ask for a disability pension at 50. At that time, disability pensions were being given to "blind" people who, once they became "officially" invalid and started receiving an invalidity pension, would drive trucks or play in soccer teams. This was not just an Italian problem. It was also a common European problem, until controls became more effective in later years. However, the problem continues and, in 2010, five per cent of the Italian population was receiving invalidity pensions that absorbed about one per cent of the Italian GDP.

The night before the conference in Lisbon I decided to go to the National Theater, that is located right in the middle of the city's historical center. The historical center of Lisbon in the 18th century had been largely destroyed by an earthquake. It had been rebuilt and it is now a very attractive area. The theater was advertising a special program of modern dance called "Dance Before You Think." The title made me curious so I bought a ticket for the evening show. The dance turned out to be the silliest I had ever seen. For some reason the stage was full of dead fish (sardines) and the female dancer would make movements that to me were totally lacking of any grace or meaning. I thought that it would have been good if the dancer would think before dancing. Spontaneity can be a problem at times, especially when it is not accompanied by grace.

Fortunately that afternoon I had gone back to visit the Gulbenkian Museum and had once again admired its rich collection that included paintings by Rembrandt, Rubens, various French impressionists and splendid pieces of oriental and middle eastern ceramics, Italian tapestries, and much more. A Portuguese friend, Manuel Sebastian, had invited me for lunch at *Tagide*, a very nice restaurant with fantastic food and a beautiful view of the Cathedral and of City Hall. This had made up for the silly dance.

The conference in which I participated was part of the so-called "North-South Dialogue." It was a high-level affair, and I was delighted and flattered that I had been invited. There were two current prime ministers, Cavaco Silva and Janez Drnovzek of Slovania; several presidential candidates or candidates for prime minister, including Kim Dae-Jung from Korea and Victor Orban from Hungary; and other important political personalities such as Arthur Dunkel, then the head of GATT, the predecessor to the World Trade Organization; Count Otto Graff Lambdorff, leader of a major political party in Germany; and Princess Maria Teresa Borbon Parma, a professor of political science in Madrid and a relative of the Spanish King. The only economists were Jagdish Bhagwati and myself.

The meeting took place in a villa, the Quinta de Ribafria, in Sintra, a beautiful, small historical town not far from Lisbon that in 1995 was awarded UNESCO's World Heritage Status. The participants were taken from their hotel in Lisbon to Sintra by bus with police escort. A problem was that the bus was often much too big for the narrow streets that it had to follow. Thus the sirens of the police escorts did not help much in making the bus move faster.

In the long bus ride I was sitting next to the Korean participant. I had no idea who he was but we engaged in a polite conversation, exchanged business cards and, over the following years, I received Christmas cards from this gentleman. I was, thus, surprised to learn later that he was a very famous man. Kim Dae-Jung became President of Korea, from 1998 to 2003, and won the Nobel Peace Prize in 2000 for trying to bring peace between the two Koreas. While he was president, he inaugurated the "sunshine policy" toward North Korea, in an attempt to establish relations with the North and promote the unification of the two Koreas. Before becoming president of Korea he had been a major opposition leader when Korea was a dictatorship, under General Park Chung-hee. He had been jailed and had narrowly escaped death, after being kidnapped in Japan by Korean agents. The CIA had intervened and had saved him. Kim Dae-jung died in September 2009. Unfortunately, his presidency was damaged by accusations of corruption and two of his sons were jailed for receiving bribes.

In the bus I also exchanged a few words with the gentleman from Hungary who was much younger than the rest of the group and was sitting on my other side. He would soon win the Hungarian elections and become prime minister. Victor Orban would again become prime minister of Hungary in 2010.

Prime Minister Cavaco Silva gave a beautiful reception and a luncheon at the historical villa. I was seated next to the Spanish Princess and had a pleasant conversation with her. I mentioned that a Borbon had been King of the area of Italy where I was born. The kingdom of Naples came to an end when Italy was unified during the Risorgimento, and the Savoy King of Piedmont became king of Italy. The Princess related the story of one of the Borbons who had been lost at sea when he was very young and that might have been saved and might have become a Maharaja in India. Apparently this particular Maharaja looked more Spanish than Indian and knew details of the Borbon family that only a family member would know.

The meeting itself was interesting. I always found these multidisciplinary meetings more stimulating than those made up exclusively of economists, which often tend to be too dry and too technical. The cross-fertilization of ideas is very important, especially today when much of economics has become too theoretical and, in the view of many, often somewhat detached from the real world. It aims to explain more and more about an invented, "virtual," world, and less and less about the actual world we live in. But I recognize that technical progress makes specialization necessary. However, it may also lead to the situation once described by a cynic where: "we learn more and more about less and less until we know everything about nothing." I am concerned that society may be putting excessive resources in the technical papers that modern-day economists write while ignoring the more practical side of economics, which still drives policies and policymakers. The incentives in the profession encourage the abstract, technical work and discourage the more mundane, practical work.

What is happening to economics reminds me a little of the Soviet Union where it was said that capital was produced simply to create more capital. There was little spillover into consumption, the output that really mattered to the population. Economic theory is producing more theory but not enough is filtering down into good policy. The distance between those who make the theories and those who make the policies seems to be getting wider. As in medicine, most economists are becoming specialists in some small areas of economics and few are working as general economists who can better see the connections between the various areas. Within the academic profession the generalists are seen as "jacks of all trades," lacking depth. Similar views have been expressed recently by those who have questioned why economists failed to see that the policies that were being pursued by major countries, and especially by the USA in the years before 2008, would likely lead to the financial crisis of 2008–2009. Even the Queen of England asked this question. There were, of course, the expected, defensive responses on the part of some economists, including one by Bob Lucas in *The Economist.*

Let me return to the conference. The first speaker was Adam Michink, a journalist from Poland. I will relate his intervention in some detail because I found it interesting. He introduced himself as an "anti-communist *par excellence*," one who had spent three years in jail and had been detained "hundreds of times" by the communist government of Poland because of his views. He said that he was the editor-in-chief of the first independent newspaper in Poland and was going to talk about "civil society." He stated that under totalitarianism individuals did not exist *as individuals.* They were state property; they were slaves of the state. The state could do whatever it wanted with them. He went on asserting that democracy required more than individual freedom. It required free institutions. Thus, a country could have free individuals but it might not have truly free institutions. He claimed that in Poland in 1993 there was individual freedom but not democratic or free institutions. He argued that in Japan, on the other hand, there was democracy without individual freedom because individuals were hesitant to diverge from the consensus that developed within the groups to which they belonged. There is no democracy without the legal framework for it and that framework is made up of free institutions.

He went on to discuss the importance of the role of the state and the idea of a nation. Should the idea of a nation be inclusive or exclusive? Should Poland be the Poland of the Poles? What about the Jews, the Russians, and the other ethnic groups living there? Should Poland be for Catholics? What about non-Catholics living in Poland? He mentioned the danger of a nation that is based on ethnic concepts or on religious concepts, when national frontiers do not reflect these concepts. Ethnic nations inevitably lead to aggression against those within the nation who do not belong to the national ethnic group. He claimed to be the main person in Poland defending the rights of the Russian Poles and of Gypsies and Jews. He thought that this was ironic because he had fought the Russians for decades. In a nation based on ethnic concepts there was the danger that other ethnic groups (Russians, Gypsies, Jews) would end up being blamed for everything, including most crimes. He asserted that the Catholic Church, that had led the fight against communism, was now leading the fight for the establishment of Catholic values and not civic values. He asked whether this was a first step towards a new form of totalitarianism.

In post-communist Eastern Europe, as in many other areas of the world, all frontiers are unjust in some sense. This fact, combined with the ethnic concept of the state, leads to inevitable conflicts. There is evidence of this all over the world. Many of the chaotic situations that developed in recent years (Iraq, Rwanda, East Timor, Congo) to some extent reflect the conflict outlined by Adam Michink. Even the Israeli-Palestinian conflict is partly based on the problems created by an ethnic-based concept of state.

Michink moved from politics to economics, and I felt that here he was on shakier ground. He argued that economic liberalism requires a change of mentality. He admitted that a market economy is a *sine qua non* for a civic society. But, he argued, the idea of a market economy was being degraded by those who wanted to use "Pinochet methods" to bring it. This was the imposition of a market economy through non-democratic means. He saw the danger of liberal economic ideas "with a Pinochet face." In a clear reference to Leszek Balcerowicz, the liberal minister of economics in Poland at the time, who would become the President of the Central Bank, he claimed that "Chicago boys" were pushing liberal economic ideas regardless of their political implications. In Michink's view, liberal economic policies had become justifications for non-democratic political organizations. I had difficulty in understanding this last point which conflicted with much economic thinking that argues that liberal economics generates more political freedom.

Princess Borbon Parma gave a nice talk on the need for understanding Islamic movements, explaining that it was a natural instinct of human beings to organize themselves in communities or groups around religious, ethnic, or ideological criteria. In many cases these groups have more cohesion than those which just relate to a nation. This made me think of *campanilismo* in Italy, which is allegiance to towns and not to the country, and of the famous statement by Massimo D'Azeglio, an Italian policymaker, that "we have made Italy; now we must make the Italians." Italians continue to relate themselves more to their campanile (bell tower), or to the town where they were born, or their province, than to their country. Because in Italy there are 8,000 municipalities, there are potentially 8,000 versions of Italy, which makes governing very difficult. The Princess argued that it was important to have tolerance for other groups and to maintain links with them. She seemed particularly concerned about what she saw as attempts toward demonization of Islam. Because the Conference was taking place in 1993, this observation showed remarkable foresight.

The Secretary General of GATT (The General Agreement on Tariff and Trade), the predecessor to the WTO (World Trade Organization) gave his characteristically forceful presentation in which he decried what he called the new "iron curtain" that was being drawn between Eastern and Western Europe. In the West, the curtain was driven by fear, in the East by frustration. He said that people, and especially politicians, did not understand that free trade is not about the sharing of the cake but about its size. For this reason it is important to keep explaining the virtue of free trade. The problem is that people accept free trade in theory but not in practice. He related that Helmut Kohl, then the Prime Minister of Germany, had told him that when he met representatives of specific industries, they spent two thirds of the time expounding on the virtue of free trade and the remaining third explaining why their industry must be the exception. Dunkel argued that the world had changed. While in the past it was the industrial countries that defended free trade, now it was the developing countries. He predicted that it would be difficult to conclude the Uruguay round of trade liberalization on the basis of the existing agenda that included requests for many special preferences. Here again these illustrated great foresight.

Dunkel expressed concern about the Clinton administration that had recently started to use world trade as an instrument to impose its own ethical standards and social rules on other countries. There was a great danger for developing countries when American labor standards are imposed on much poorer countries. Some even argued that workers in very poor countries that exported to the United States should be paid the same wages as American workers, a silly idea that has been around for a long time. In Dunkel's view, this would deprive workers in poorer countries of jobs and would make it much more difficult for developing countries to reduce poverty. He concluded that bilateral trade agreements between countries are not the solution, free trade is. The bilateral trade agreements have created a "spaghetti bowl" of bilateral arrangements. These trade arrangements may be distracting the policymakers from the important goal of promoting *general*, free trade.

Dunkel's comments on labor standards reminded me of a column written several decades ago by Milton Friedman, I believe in *Business Week*, in which he mentioned that he owed his education to the sweat shops that labor leaders wanted to abolish in poor countries. He reported that when he was a child his mother had worked in one of these sweat shops in New York. This was the only job available to her and had allowed her to feed the family. The income she earned was low and the working conditions were terrible. But the alternative had been no job, which would have meant starvation or recourse to illegal activities. Without the job in the sweat shop for his mother, Milton Friedman would not have been able to study and become a Nobel Prize winner and one of the most influential economists of the 20th century.

Another interesting intervention, which also showed a lot of foresight, was that of a reporter from the *Times of India*, Swaminatham Aiyar, who discussed the growth over time in the power of the individual compared to the power of the state, especially in democratic, market-oriented nations. The growing power of individuals was the result of freedom of movements, combined with the use of new technology and rising incomes, which allowed individuals to better exploit that freedom. In comparison the state was becoming progressively weaker. He referred to terrorist acts that had occurred a few months before the conference, which was taking place in April 1993. These terrorist acts were the first bombing at the World Trade Center in New York, and the bombings of the City of London and at the stock exchange in Bombay (Mumbai). Much worse acts would come later, including the destruction of the World Trade Center on September 11, 2001 and the occupation of the Taj Hotel in Mumbai in 2008. Both of these acts reflected the growing power of individuals to do harm to others. He asked whether terrorism would affect the role of the state and force the state to restrict individual freedom.

This question became of greater interest in later years when some states, including the United States under President Bush, tried to respond to acts of terrorism by (a) increasing the power of the state in some areas, and (b) reducing to some extent the freedom of individuals. The use of the Patriot Act in the United States and the jailing and torturing of individuals without proper trials has been interpreted by many observers exactly in these terms. It has increased the power of the state vis-à-vis that of the individual. That increased state power has been seen as a natural or inevitable response to terrorism. But, it implies that the more terrorism there will be, the more the state will want to increase its relative power respect to that of individuals. Only time will tell where this kind of transition will lead.

Changes may be gradual, and thus may not elicit strong reactions when they take place. Some may even support or justify these changes. But, at the end of the day, we may find that the freedom that we have enjoyed over the years, including many rights to privacy, may become things of the past. For example, full body scanners at airports may become routine tools. Some central tenets of a market economy, such as free trade, free movement of capital, free movement of persons, may suffer the consequences of terrorism and of making the state more politically powerful as a reaction to it. Over the long run security may become a more important government objective, compared to individual freedom. History indicates that when security is compromised, people are willing to give up on some of their political freedoms. At some point, if terrorism continues, and seems to be a great danger, the difference between democracy and authoritarianism may become smaller. This may be a transition in the wrong direction. Let us hope that we never experience it in full.

A final intervention that merits a mention was that of Count Lambsdorff, then the leader of the Federal Democratic Party, FDP, in Germany. He commented on the importance of good economic advisers for heads of government. He specifically mentioned that Adenauer, the German Prime Minister after World War Two, had been lucky to have had Dr. Ludwig Erhard as his economic adviser. Heads of governments often do not have an economic preparation and at times they come to power with ideas that may not be the best. One is reminded of Keynes's famous statement about dead economists influencing current economic policy. Thus, what they need are economic advisers that brief them properly; not advisers who become advocates of their own preconceived ideas or their vested interests; or who try to provide support for the leaders' bad ideas.

Listening to this comment, I could not help thinking about the role that Walter Heller had played in educating President Kennedy. Heller's book *New Dimensions of Political Economy*, published in 1966, is still worth reading. Unfortunately when heads of governments are guided by strong ideologies, be they good or bad, they prefer to surround themselves with advocates rather than advisers. Ideology drives out analysis, because the ideology itself is assumed to provide the answers, thus dispensing with the need to analyze problems. This point was forcefully made in Ron Suskind's *The Price of Loyalty*, the book on Paul O'Neill's experience in the Bush Administration. O'Neill was the first Treasury Secretary in the Bush Administration. A man of great experience and impeccable conservative views, he was forced out because he was not considered to be loyal enough to the prevailing ideology.

My own intervention had to do with the role that international institutions could play in fighting world poverty. It must not have been very profound because I do not recall much of what I said and I did not keep any notes on my own remarks.

I went back to Lisbon in August 1995 to attend the Annual Congress of the International Institute of Public Finance (IIPF). I had been president of the IIPF from 1990 to 1994 and had presided over the commemoration of the 50th Anniversary of the creation of the Institute, at Harvard University in 1994. The local host for the Lisbon meeting was Professor Antonio Pinto Barbosa of the Universidade Nova. Professor Peter Birch Sorensen, from Denmark, was the Chairman of the Scientific Committee. The chosen theme for the congress was "The Changing Role of the Government in the Economy." It was a theme that I would pursue in my own research in later years.

Professor Anibal Cavaco Silva opened the meeting by paying tribute to two of the grand old men of public finance, Richard Musgrave and Alan Peacock, who were attending the meeting. When I was a graduate student at Harvard in the early 1960s, they had been considered towering figures in the field of public finance.

Musgrave, who had been the more influential of the two, was an advocate of "normative" public finance, the economics that tells a good government what it should do, using taxes and public spending as instruments, to promote good policies and the welfare of the citizens. He had popularized the concept of the role of the government in three separate branches: allocation of resources, redistribution of income, and stabilization of the economy. This way of thinking about the role of the state had great influence on students and practitioners of public finance and influenced a whole generation of scholars. It also placed a lot of confidence on the intention and capacity of governments to promote good policies. I found Musgrave's trust in the ability and willingness of governments to solve economic problems and to improve the citizen's welfare a bit puzzling, partly because of Musgrave's background and partly because of my work with many governments that made me question that trust. Musgrave was born and raised in Germany and had moved to the United States in the thirties, during Hitler's time. In view of this background, it was commendable that he had retained this great trust in the actions of governments.

Peacock had had more influence on what came to be called "public choice," a school of thought that had developed predominantly in the United States, especially under the influence of James Buchanan who would get a Nobel Prize in Economics for his contribution to the creation of that school. The school of public choice recognized that governments make mistakes and assumed that these are not just random or honest mistakes. It believes that it is difficult for policymakers to escape the influence that personal and other special interests have on them. The school assumes that politicians are products of their influences. Their policies are impacted by lobbies, politics, corruption and other influences or biases. Thus, in some ways, Peacock's approach was more grounded in reality. In the Italian "*Scienza delle Finanze*" that had flourished in Italy between 1880 and 1940, that approach had been prevalent. Musgrave's approach provided more easily developed, normative, recommendations for policymakers, and, because of this, it was a useful reference for an economic adviser. Peacock's approach was more useful for explaining outcomes of policies. Peacock had co-authored, with Jack Wiseman, an influential book in which he had argued that wars lead to permanent increases in public spending.

The first plenary session of the conference had three papers. The first, by Richard Musgrave, was a thoughtful overview of the historical role of the state in the economy. The second, by Hans-Werner Sinn, a leading German economist from Munich, dealt with the role of insurances in the distribution and redistribution of income. The third was my paper on the role of the state and the control that governments have over policy instruments. In this paper I emphasized the role of regulations as policy instruments that often substitute taxes and public spending. Until the 2008–2009 crisis regulations had received relatively little attention on the part of public finance economists who had concentrated on taxes and public expenditure. I explained that frequently governments attempt to achieve with regulations what they could more efficiently achieve with spending or taxing. The reason is that there are less political obstacles to the use of regulations. For this reason they tend to be abused. At the same time the regulators may be captured by the regulated so that the regulations may not have the intended results.

After the session I was invited to a lunch at the Prime Minister's official residence together with a few participants, most of whom had attended the University of York that in the fifties and sixties had been a major public finance center, and had provided the main competition to Harvard in public finance. I was in the minority of persons at the luncheon who had not studied at York and felt almost embarrassed by this perceived shortcoming.

I was happy to see Cavaco Silva's charming wife, Maria, and their son. Eight years as prime minister had not changed him or his family. He continued to be very friendly and courteous. I recalled that the last time I had been their dinner guest they were living in a modest apartment. Now they were living in a large, beautiful, official residence, but that had not changed their friendliness and their attitude.

During the luncheon the Prime Minister reminisced about heads of governments' meetings that he had attended during the past eight years. He mentioned that his term would soon end and that he planned to go back to teaching and writing. He recalled one time being seated, because of alphabetical order, next to Margaret Thatcher, the British Prime Minister, who seemed to love being in the minority of one. This must have given her the feeling of being unique. He related an interesting story on how Giulio Andreotti, then Prime Minister of Italy, might have contributed to the political downfall of Mrs. Thatcher. He related that, at one of these prime ministers' meetings chaired by Andreotti, she was continuously and forcefully objecting, taking extreme positions vis-à-vis issues concerning the European Union. Rather than adjusting the text of the concluding statement to accommodate her objections and views, Andreotti chose to put all her statements in footnotes. This choice highlighted how extreme her views were, compared to those of other heads of governments, and how isolated she was. This led to the resignation of the British foreign secretary, Douglas Hurd, which in turn led to her fall. He also commented that President George H. W. Bush was the most friendly head of state he had met, especially vis-à-vis the Prime Minister of a small and relatively poor country as was Portugal.

His comment about Andreotti reminded me of a time when I was in a plane going from Rome to New York. I was seated in the first class, upper section, of a 747 Boeing on an Alitalia flight, at a time when IMF employees traveled in first class. The remaining seats were all taken by Prime Minister Andreotti and by various assistants who were accompanying him to some meeting in the United States. He had ordered something (I believe a scarf) from the duty free and had paid in lire. Sometime later he had discovered that he had been overcharged, because of the wrong foreign exchange rate used, and asked the stewardess to have the small difference reimbursed. Obviously there had been an honest mistake on the part of the Alitalia flight attendant who seemed to be surprised and embarrassed. The episode was descriptive of this man who was no fool and had the reputation of being as clever as a fox. He was Italian Prime Minister seven times, had written several books, was reported to be very religious, had been accused and absolved of having ordered the murder of a reporter, and of having had ties to the Sicilian Mafia, and is now one of five "senators for life" in the Italian Senate.

When I became undersecretary in the Italian government (2001–2003) and had to represent the Italian government in the Senate, I admired Andreotti's interventions. They were always interesting, precise, and relevant. A recent award-winning movie, *Il Divo*, directed by Paolo Sorentino, has reported on the colorful life and political career of this interesting and unusual man. Toni Servillo gives an extraordinary performance as Giulio Andreotti in the movie. The message of the movie seems to be that Andreotti's life and actions typified Machiavelli's maxim, that the ends justify the means. Sometimes evil actions, or actions perceived as being evil, are pursued in the interest of the good. The point of the movie seems to be that whatever actions Andreotti may have pursued, he was convinced that he was doing it for the good of Italy.

On the second day of the meeting, the participants were taken on an excursion to a farm outside of Lisbon where a performance by superbly trained horses had been arranged. The performance was fantastic. I was not aware that horses could be trained to do all these tricks. I was told that they belonged to a special breed of Portuguese horses.

Towards the end of the conference a special article in *Diario de Noticias* discussed papers presented by Professors Musgrave and Phelps and by myself. Professor Phelps, who was also attending the conference, would receive the Nobel Prize in economics in later years. I was interviewed for a long article to be published in *Exame*, a monthly business magazine. I had lunch with Miguel Beleza, the economist who had bought the Rolex in 1975 to protect his savings from the feared takeover by the communists and lost it to a thief. By this time he had been governor of the Central Bank of Portugal and had had the almost inevitable debate with the Minister of Finance, who was Jorge Braga de Machedo, on the proper level of the domestic discount rate. As is normally the case, the minister wanted lower interest rates than the governor thought it was proper. Ministers of Finance want an easier time, during their normally short, political time horizon, to service the public debt or to stimulate the economy, while Central Bank Governors worry more about longer-term price stability. This divergence is a constant in the political economy of countries. In recent years, with the creation of the European Central Bank, the pressures to lower the discount rate in European countries were transferred to the European Central Bank. The 2008–2009 "Great Recession" proved that Central Banks are perfectly able to play the role of Santa Claus on a large scale, with their off-budget and, largely fiscal, actions. Thus, the sharp separation, between fiscal and monetary policies, found in textbook, is somewhat artificial. It does not reflect reality.

I went back to Portugal in May 1997, to attend a seminar on corruption. This was the first seminar organized by the IMF on a topic that had been taboo in the past within that institution. The IMF had finally recognized corruption as a potential, major, economic problem for countries. I was happy about this development because I had been trying for years to open the eyes of that institution to this growing problem. A paper I had written in 1993, presented at a conference on the "Economics of Organized Crime," held in Bologna (Italy), had started raising the Fund's awareness to this problem. The paper by the title of "Corruption: Arm's-length Relationship, and Markets" was published in 1995, by Cambridge University Press, in a volume carrying the same title as the conference. The Bologna Conference had taken place in a very tense environment. It was held a few days after the Mafia had bombed the Uffizi Gallery in Florence in a campaign of bombing aimed at changing some government policies vis-à-vis organized crime. Several foreign participants had been scared about participating in a conference that would discuss organized crime and its connection to corruption. Some American participants had even backed out of it at the last moment. One of the Italian participants, Luciano Violante, was, at the time, the head of the Anti-Mafia Commission in the Italian Parliament. He went around being constantly accompanied by a police escort. Because of these developments the conference had been held almost in secrecy, due to concern that organized crime might attempt to disrupt it.

In a different, revised version that stressed the corruption part of it and deleted the organized crime part, the Bologna paper was discussed at a retreat with executive directors of the IMF that Michel Camdessus, the Fund's Managing Director at that time, organized in June 1996. Camdessus had been much concerned about corruption, and aware of its nefarious effects, but he had been reluctant to speak up and implicitly or explicitly criticize the policymakers of some countries who were, after all, the masters of the Fund. In the mid-1990s, the growing attention that the American government was giving to this topic gave him cover so that he felt freer to broach the subject within the Fund. It was becoming clear that corruption was not just a political problem but also a major economic problem that could have macro-economic implication for some countries.

At the beginning there were the usual negative reactions from some of the Fund's executive directors who represented the countries and even from regular IMF staff members. The executive directors complained that attention to corruption would make the Fund engage more in the internal affairs of countries that should be none of its business. The Fund's regular staff argued that this would take the institution away from its traditional mandate, that was macroeconomic stability and would create some frictions between Fund staff and the authorities of some countries. Some maintained that corruption had nothing to do with macroeconomic developments. This refrain had become the refuge of those who never wanted to change anything. Several experiences in countries such as Kenya, Russia, Argentina, Ivory Coast, Cambodia, Gabon, Zaire, and others had suggested that corruption (a) was a big problem, and (b) it often had macroeconomic consequences, when large amounts of money ended up in the Swiss bank accounts of corrupt leaders; or when politically-backed, bad investments were made because of bribes paid to some government officials. Ignoring it weakened the fundamental role of the Fund. Therefore, there were good reasons for the Fund to pay attention to this problem. Mr. Camdessus, then the Fund's Managing Director, became a strong advocate of the fight against corruption. At the same time, the President of the World Bank, Mr.Wolfensohn, had also joined the fight against this phenomenon.

By coincidence, the week when I arrived in Portugal for the seminar on corruption, President Mobutu had been thrown out of Zaire, where corruption had been a major issue. A long article in the *Financial Times* the previous week had linked Mobutu's reign to corruption. Later articles in the *Wall Street Journal* had raised questions about the role of the IMF in Zaire. The IMF had kept lending money to the country when it was obvious that major corruption was going on and that the Fund money was not being used for the intended purpose. The role of the Fund in these affairs had been somewhat embarrassing. The institution had been aware, but had ignored the fact, that a line in Zaire's budget, called "dotation du president," a special budgetary allowance for the president, had been increasing significantly over the years and had reached the extraordinary level of six percent of GDP. The Fiscal Affairs Department within the IMF had raised questions about this line item in the budget and about its growth, but its questions had been ignored mainly because the IMF was not supposed to comment on the composition of the budget but only on the fiscal deficit. A 707 jet, used by Mobutu, had been impounded at the airport of Lisbon because it had not paid airport fees.

The *Financial Times* story reported that Mobutu loved Port wine and, given his refined taste, drank only Port at least as old as his age. At the time I went to Portugal for this seminar, Port that old cost over U.S. $1,000 a bottle. Obviously, as he got older the cost of the Port he drank increased progressively. There was the question of how much money Mobutu had abroad. Billions of U.S. dollars were mentioned because he had appropriated billions of U.S. dollars over the years. However, it was more difficult to assess how much he still had, given his expensive habits and given the cost of staying in power in Zaire for which he had to buy the services (if not the allegiance) of very demanding individuals. It had been reported in the media that he had bought the services of a political opponent for U.S. $5 million. He had also tried, unsuccessfully, to buy the support of some Fund staff members who were dealing with him.

The seminar in Lisbon had been organized for participants from Lusophone and other African countries and had been financed by the French Ministry of Technical Cooperation and by the Portuguese Central Bank. The participants were for the most part at the rank of minister of finance, governor of central bank, or director general of finance or of customs.

At the beginning of the conference the participants were wary. The questions in their minds must have been: Why was I invited? Why was my country chosen? Why is the Fund interested in corruption? Some of these questions were articulated in an indirect way. After a while, the participants relaxed. The director of customs of the Ivory Coast, a country where a recent technical assistance mission from my department had not been able to account for many millions of dollars of customs revenue, declared categorically that there was no corruption at customs in his country. A lively discussion followed on corruption in financial markets, in tax administration, in customs, in government procurements, and in public investments, often the most sensitive areas with respect to this problem. It became clear that bribes could change some innocent-looking public sector actions to bring advantages to particular groups. For example, the bank where the government kept its uncompensated, cash deposits was much benefited by this action. It did not have to pay interest on that deposit and could use the money for making its loans.

At the end of the conference, in the afternoon, a couple of colleagues and I went to an area called San Bento to look at antiques. They were terribly expensive and the shops were completely empty of people. I wondered who bought this stuff at these prices. In the evening my Portuguese friend, Manuel Sebastian, invited me to a restaurant by the sea in Cascais called Ponto Santa Maria. We had a nice dinner with grilled fish, fried cod and a marvelous, soft, goat cheese called *queijo da serra* (mountain cheese). Manuel, an employee of the Central Bank, was involved at that time in the design of the Euro bills and coins in anticipation of the introduction of the Euro. Portugal would become part of the European Monetary Union. A committee with representatives from the European Union's member countries was meeting regularly to agree on the final design of the coins and the paper money. Like everything else in the European

Union, the agreement was proving difficult. He related some of the politics that was going into it. For example the Spaniards were insisting to have their islands shown in the maps of Europe. However, the relative proportions of those islands rendered them invisible.

I came away from this trip with the impression that Portugal was still a relatively poor country but was making significant progress moving away from its past and truly rejoining Europe. It was a transition that would take time to be complete but the direction was the right one.

I went back to Lisbon in November 2004 to participate in a conference organized by the Portuguese Fiscal Association. The conference was to commemorate the Portuguese tax reform and to honor Professor Paulo Pitta e Cunha who had been instrumental in it. I went there with my wife and we were put in a new, elegant Hotel called Pestana Palace. The hotel had taken over a palace built at the beginning of the 20th century by a Portuguese who had made a large fortune in Africa and had lent a lot of money to the king of Portugal. The palace had been built near the Royal Palace to evidence the relationship of the palace owner to the king. Unfortunately for its owner, soon after the completion of the palace the king was thrown out, reducing the location and prestige value of the palace. It had remained empty for many years until it was transformed in a luxury hotel.

At the conference I saw old friends and met new ones, including especially Dr. Eduardo Paz Ferreiro and his charming, Angolan-born wife, Francisca, who is a judge in the Portuguese justice system. He was the President of the Portuguese Fiscal Association, the association that had invited me. I participated in a round table with Dr. Silva Lopez, the former Governor of the Central Bank, Dr. Braga de Macedo, the former Minister of Finance and a couple other people. I spoke about "fiscal termites," a theme that I was pursuing in some of my writing, starting with a paper I had presented in 1996 at a meeting of the German Economic Association. My thesis was that various developments going on at that time, largely connected with the phenomenon of globalization and with important technological developments, were making it progressively more difficult for countries to continue collecting high tax levels. My 1996 article had inspired a cover story in the *Economist* with the title of the "Disappearing Taxpayer." The image of the termites that were eating away at the foundations of the tax systems helped dramatize this trend.

By 2004 Portugal had contributed Mr. José Manuel Barroso to the European Commission as the new president, following Mr. Romano Prodi. However, the country was undergoing a difficult economic period especially because of high public spending that could not be financed with tax revenue. The fiscal deficit had substantially exceeded the limit imposed by the "Stability and Growth Pact" of the Maastrict Treaty. Unfortunately, fiscal problems would continue in the following years and in 2010 Portugal would face serious fiscal difficulties. Thus, the transition away from an inflated role of the state would still be a long way from completion.

I went back to Lisbon in November 2005 to receive an Honorary Degree from the University of Lisbon. This trip took place during the political campaign to choose the next president of Portugal. It would result in Dr. Cavaco Silva becoming President. Getting to Lisbon in time to participate in the ceremony that would award the honorary degree to me and three other candidates turned out to be very difficult. The morning of the day I was supposed to leave for Lisbon I got an e-mail from the travel agent in Lisbon that had issued my electronic plane ticket informing me that my flight (on Continental airlines) from Washington to Newark airport that afternoon had been cancelled. Because the flight to Lisbon (from Newark) was in the evening I did not worry. There was ample time to get to Newark from Washington. I called Continental airline to confirm the cancellation of the Washington–Newark flight and to be put on another flight. I was kept on the phone for at least half an hour and then I was informed that there was no way they could get me to the Newark airport on that day. I was annoyed and decided to go to Newark by train. The train took only three hours and made a convenient stop at the Newark Airport, where I would get the flight (on Continental) for Lisbon. When my wife and I reported to the counter of Continental Airlines in Newark, more than two hours before the departure of the plane for Lisbon, I was informed that our seats had been given to others because of the canceling of the Washington–Newark flight in the morning. I was *very* upset. After a lot of discussion with a supervisor, we were put on a flight to Madrid from where we could get a connection to Lisbon. I got to the University of Lisbon in the middle of the ceremony, just in time to receive the degree. I swore that I would never fly again with Continental Airlines. There was no excuse for its behavior.

In more recent years I have gone to Lisbon a few more times mainly to participate in activities organized by the Portuguese

Fiscal Associations. By this time Portugal had become just one of the European, peaceful democracies, with an inflated public sector and with continuing fiscal problems. However, it had not lost its charm. If anything the city has acquired more charm. At the time of this writing, July 2010, Portugal is in the middle of the fiscal crisis that started in Greece. It has had its own credit rating downgraded by two notches and no one knows when that crisis will stop, or how far it will spread.

Chapter 10

Somalia: The Slaughterhouse and the Sharks

In the summer of 1979 the IMF received an urgent request from the Somali government to send a mission that would help improve tax collection. At the time, the public finances of Somalia were in a disastrous state and the country was experiencing a period of high inflation. Somalia had become closely linked with the governments of centrally planned economies from which it was getting policy advice and some financial help. There was some hope in Washington that, if assisted, it might begin to follow more market-friendly policies and get closer to the West. I was asked to lead a Fund mission that would include four other IMF staff members.

In late August, the International Institute of Public Finance (IIPF), held its annual congress that I often attended, so I decided to combine the two activities in one trip in order to save travel expenses and travel time. The IIPF Congress that year was taking place in Taormina, Sicily, which is on the way from Washington to Somalia, making it easier to combine the two trips.

I arrived at the hotel in Taormina, where the congress would take place, late at night and was told that all the rooms were full. They had given my reserved room to someone else because of my late arrival. After some discussion with the staff of the hotel and the presentation of my American passport, I was given the presidential suite! I later joked that, after the movie *The Godfather* had come out, an American passport with a name of Vito in it carried much weight in Sicily! I settled comfortably in the presidential suite in the splendid environment offered by Taormina, originally a Greek town near the Etna volcano. The town is located in one of the most spectacular natural settings in the World. It has been a major tourist attraction for a long time. Winston Churchill used to spend some vacations days there. Taormina has even a beautiful Indian garden built by a very rich English woman who had lived in India and had fallen in love with this city. She had taken a bit of India with her to Taormina. The Greco-Roman theatre, with an incredible view of the Etna, provides one of the most stunning settings anywhere on Earth.

Some prominent economists and public finance experts attended the IIPF Congress. Professor Giuseppe Sobbrio, of the University of

Messina, and Professor Francesco Forte, of the University of Torino, had been instrumental in organizing it and had done a very good job. I shared a panel with Professor John Hicks, from the United Kingdom, who was one of the earliest winners of the Nobel Prizes in economics. Both of our papers dealt with the definition of income which was and has remained an important topic in economics. My paper dealt with the measurement of the income of enterprises in an inflationary context. At the time this was a hot topic because of high inflation in several advanced countries, including the United States. How does an enterprise account for the replacement costs of the goods sold (or the inputs used to produce them) when there is high inflation? Should the cost of depreciable assets and of stocks used be adjusted for inflation? Enterprises generally did not make such adjustments and the tax systems did not allow them. Furthermore, if an adjustment is justified, should it reflect the changes in the *general* price level, or should it reflect the inflation in the *specific* categories of assets used? This issue was also highly relevant for the calculation of capital gains on the sale of assets such as houses. I argued in favor of inflation adjustment and of using indexes of inflation that reflected the price changes of specific categories and not the general price changes.

While I was in Taormina, I developed a health problem that led me to consult a local doctor. The glands around my neck had become swollen, indicating that I had some kind of infection. I asked the doctor whether he thought that I could proceed to Somalia, in view of my health problem. He prescribed some antibiotics and strongly advised me to cancel my trip, commenting that I would not like to get ill and end up in a hospital in Mogadishu. However, it would have been difficult at this point to cancel the trip because I was the head of the Somali mission and the other members of the mission had already left Washington and were on the way to Mogadishu. At a time when cellular phones still did not exist, it would have been impossible to reach them. Furthermore, the prevailing culture of the IMF strongly discouraged the cancellation of mission trips. Thus, I decided to take my chances and proceed as planned. Fortunately, the antibiotics worked and I did not have health problems during the mission.

To get to Mogadishu, I had to fly to Beirut, where I would take a flight with Middle Eastern Airlines, MEA, for Mogadishu. At the time, Lebanon was in the middle of a civil war but, remarkably, the Beirut airport was still open and MEA was still flying. I did not much like the idea of going through Beirut and of spending some hours at its airport, but alternative routes to Somalia were much more complex. Well, apart from the concern of being blown up at the airport of Beirut, or being hijacked on the way to Somalia, which at the time was also a concrete possibility, the trip was okay. At the Beirut airport I met my Fund colleagues, and we all proceeded for Mogadishu where we arrived at the scheduled time.

At the Mogadishu airport, we were received by the representatives of the Somali authorities that included the heads of the direct and indirect taxes and the head of the tax police. They drove us to the hotel in the center of the town where we had made reservations. The hotel was rated as the best hotel in a town not famous for comfortable hotels.

When we arrived at the hotel and asked for our reserved rooms, we were told, with a smile, "Sorry, your reservations were cancelled at the request of a minister who needed the rooms to accommodate a foreign delegation." Apparently reservations did not have much meaning in a country where it was common for ministers to request the use of rooms already reserved. Somalia was after all a "command economy" at that time so that ministers could easily "command" the use of hotel rooms. There were no other rooms available at the hotel. After some discussion and the realization that there was not much we could do in a country where the IMF did not have much leverage and where the concept of rules or respect for contracts had no meaning, we had no choice but accept the suggestion to go to another less central and, we were told, less comfortable hotel, called Jubba.

The Jubba Hotel had been recently built by the Chinese government as a gift to Somalia. Apparently China was already active in Africa at that time. In 1979 Somalia was firmly in the Soviet and Chinese sphere of influence; it had accepted the principles and was introducing the institutions of central planning. It was thus undergoing a process of transition in what could be considered the wrong direction. Private activities were discouraged and economic policy had come to reflect the Soviet model. The Jubba Hotel was Spartan and unfinished but not bad. It was also a walking distance from the center of the town. However, there were a few problems:

First, there was no restaurant or even a coffee shop in the hotel, or room service for food. This meant that all food consumption had to take place outside the hotel, which we soon discovered was not a minor problem.

Second, the hotel had an elevator but it was out of order all the time of our stay (about three weeks) and our rooms were on the fourth floor. Well, the four flights of stairs were manageable problems, since this gave us the opportunity to get some exercise.

Third, and a potentially more serious shortcoming, at each floor's landing, on the stairway, there were large openings which, like French windows, went all the way to the floor of the landing. This was nice because it provided light during the day, and fresh air. The problem was that the openings did not yet have any doors or windows. They were just open spaces. Thus, there was the risk of stepping into the opening and falling down several stories. This was especially a concern when, at night, we had to go up without the benefit of lights, because there were often blackouts.

Finally, we soon discovered that the rooms had very big and quite visible cockroaches that did not seem to be much impressed by our presence. This last problem was partly solved by the floor lady who, with a charming smile, provided us with a can of DDT with which to spray the room and our bed. Of course DDT had long disappeared from the part of the world where we came from, because of its bad effect on health! But, in a second-best world, it proved effective against the cockroaches!

To compensate for these problems, the people of the hotel were very nice and helpful. They did their best to make our stay as comfortable as it was possible, under the circumstances of a country that had become an international basket case and was moving fast toward a civil war.

During our three weeks in Somalia, the problem of eating became a major one. As I already said, the hotel had no food facilities whatsoever and most food shops in Mogadishu were mostly empty. We tried to go to the dining room of the major hotel, where we had been denied admission, and soon discovered its limitations. The first time we went, we noticed that there was a water leak from the ceiling of the large dining room. The leak was quite strong and buckets had been placed on the floor under the leak and were changed frequently when they became full. The leak had not been fixed the second time we went there and water was still falling. In fact, the leak was slowly becoming a waterfall causing the pavement of the dining room to become a little lake. But this was not the main reason why we did not go a third time. The reason was a scene that I observed and which gave the *coup de grace* to our desire to eat in this hotel. As we were waiting for a table, I saw a guest who had finished his meal and got up and left. The waiter came to the table with a towel that was stained with overuse and, before our eyes, he used the towel to clean the plate in which the departed guest had eaten. Once he had cleaned the plate enough that it looked washed, the waiter simply placed it on the table for the next guest to use.

Our search for half-decent places to eat became a big preoccupation for the mission. This was not a problem of being choosy. It was a problem of potential starvation. I recall our joy when, one day, we discovered that in a small room at the American Embassy one could have a breakfast consisting of a slice of toasted bread with melted Dutch cheese on it and a cup of bad coffee. This room was the private activity of a local employee who had found a way to increase his income. To us the Spartan breakfast was heaven. Another break came when we discovered that there was a small hotel called Croce del Sud, run by an Italian family, where we could go at night for dinner. Most nights there was just one item available even though the printed menu was a long one, probably a relic from better days. The items available could vary from a plate of spaghetti with tomatoes to grilled lobsters. The hotel was permanently fully occupied by employees of Alitalia and Fiat who rented all the rooms. In a sign of globalization, a few years later I accompanied my son Alex to an international weight lifting contest in Washington and ran into one of the teenage competitors who was speaking Italian. It turned out to be the son of the owners of Croce del Sud! The American Embassy's little room and Croce del Sud in some way solved our morning and evening eating problems. This left lunch time.

All the work in Mogadishu stopped by one o'clock. There was no work in the afternoon and all the offices closed. We discovered that there was a place by the beach called simply the "club" where the few foreigners, and especially the employees of the United Nations who lived in Mogadishu, went for lunch after the offices closed. There the standard fare was grilled fish. Because I like grilled fish, I did not mind the monotony of eating grilled fish every day for weeks. One day a member of our mission made the mistake of visiting the kitchen of the club. After that day he never ate lunch again. I preferred to be left in my comfortable ignorance and continued to eat my grilled fish. This was further proof to me that at times the truth can be harmful! I was a firm believer in the principle that if you want to continue eating sausages, do not visit the place where they make them.

Mogadishu has a magnificent beach. It is several miles long and has beautiful white sand. The beach is also very wide. It thus compares positively with most nice beaches that I have seen. I noticed, however, that, although there were always a lot of people on the beach, few if any went into the water. Those who did stayed near the shore and generally spent only a few minutes in the water. I soon discovered why. The reason was a good one. The sea was infested with sharks and quite frequently some swimmer simply disappeared, becoming lunch for the sharks. Shark teeth could be bought everywhere. There was also a good reason why there were so many sharks in the area. It seems that in their competition with China to gain political influence in Somalia, the Russians had donated a modern slaughterhouse to Somalia. The slaughterhouse had been built near the sea so that the blood from the animals could be disposed of easily and cheaply. The blood had, of course, attracted many sharks, who probably found the smell but not the substance to satisfy their hunger. Some joked that the presence of sharks was providing the solution to Somalia's population problem. The slaughterhouse provided a perfect example of what economists call an externality. That is, an activity may be a useful one, as must have been the slaughterhouse, but in the process it generates benefits or, in this case, costs that are totally unrelated to the main activity and are not reflected in the price of the product or service sold.

At that time Mogadishu was both a colorful and a depressing town. I distinctly recall the appearance of Somali women who looked like queens in their multicolored attires and carried themselves with great dignity and grace. Somehow here poverty, while real, did not seem to have the depressing appearance that I had seen elsewhere, as for example on the Indian subcontinent or in Haiti. It was somehow covered by the folklore and the colors. The city itself had some pleasant looking areas, mostly built by the Italians during their period of occupation. I was surprised and pleased to see that many Somali, and especially those more advanced in age, were happy to speak to me in Italian. This was the only Fund mission, outside of Italy, where my knowledge of Italian had turned out to be useful. In the center of the city there were still writings on walls that welcomed Mussolini's visit to Mogadishu in the 1930s. We visited the Cathedral where the representative of the Vatican praised the kindness of the Somali population but complained that in the 30 years he had been there, he had not witnessed a single conversion by Somali people to the Catholic faith.

There were many murals throughout the city, some very colorful, that graphically depicted what would happen to people who stole: their hand was shown being cut off from the arm and blood was shown dripping from the amputated arm! These pictures were everywhere, but I could not find out how frequently these punishments were effectively applied, or what effects they had on stealing. However, in a period that preceded the advent of terrorism, we felt safe and did not hesitate to walk at night without an escort. Perhaps we were simply unaware of dangers.

We had been given a car and a driver to take us around during the day. The driver was a tall, slim Somali with a bad temper who asked for money to buy cigarettes every day. We tried to give him cigarettes but he refused them, saying, rather harshly, that they were not his favorite brand. He preferred to get money to buy a drug much in use in that part of the world called *khat*. *Khat* is a plant that is chewed on one side of the mouth producing a swelling of the cheek. It also produces an amphetamine-like high. If used over long periods it can cause depression, loss of libido, and mouth cancer. It comes in different qualities, is widely used by the male population, and absorbs a large share of the income of many people. We often suspected that our driver was under the influence of this drug, especially when he would become very insistent in asking for money. In later years, the fall in the price of coffee had apparently led to a large expansion in the production of the more profitable *khat*.

In our work our main contacts were the Director of Direct Taxation, the Director of Indirect Taxation, the Head of the Tax Police, and the Head of the Statistical Office. I will never forget our first visit to Mrs. Ali, the Director of Direct Taxation. We arrived at a dilapidated building and, to get to her office we had to climb a dusty stairway full of what looked like files. The files on the stairs were the tax returns of the Somali taxpayers, mostly public enterprises! They did not seem to be kept in any particular order but had simply been placed on the stairs where they collected dust.

Mrs. Ali's large office was bare except for her desk and a couple chairs. She was a tall, pleasant lady trying to do her job under very difficult circumstances. She showed us the forms that enterprises had to fill for their tax declarations. The forms were eight pages long and had been designed by the Italians, who provided some financial and technical assistance to Somalia at that time. The forms requested all kinds of detailed information. I asked Mrs. Ali to show us an actual declaration presented by some important enterprise. When she did, we noticed that in the eight pages, only one number had been filled in. This was the income declared by the enterprise. The income was a very low figure. No other figure had been provided.

Mrs. Ali explained to us her approach to what could be called auditing. After receiving the declarations, which generally had one, low number, she invited a representative of the enterprise to come to discuss the declaration and to provide details. In these meetings she would start by saying that for sure the income of the enterprise must have been much higher than the amount declared. The representative of the enterprise would refer to the bad times and the political and economic situation and insist that the amount declared was the right one. This discussion could go on for hours during which Mrs. Ali would try to raise the declared income and the tax liability. The verbal exchange would end when the two reached an agreement on a final figure, referred to as *conguaglio* from the Italian name for this kind of agreement. Of course, no real information had gone in the determination of the taxable income.

The other director was also a striking and lively woman called Mrs. Hasha. We came to refer to her as "the tiger." It seems that women do well in these high positions in tax offices. They often have the reputation of being tough but less corrupt than men. I was often reminded of a very interesting Japanese film I had once seen called *A Taxing Woman*. It told the story of a Japanese woman tax inspector who was trying to catch tax evaders and put her life in danger in the process. Over the years I have heard of several cases where women have risked their lives in trying to do an honest job as tax inspectors.

In this mission we learned some interesting things on how economic relations can affect tax revenue. We learned, for example, that the Central Bank of Somalia would lend money directly to public enterprises, presumably by printing money. The enterprises would buy capital equipment and, as was the praxis in centrally planned economies, they would be allowed to take a very small, annual depreciation allowance against this equipment. Thus, the government would tax most of what in market economies would be depreciation allowances, as if they were regular income. The rationale was that all replacement of depreciated capital had to be decided, at a central level, by the government and not by the enterprise. Thus, in a way the Central Bank would finance the government but indirectly, by artificially increasing the taxable base. Without understanding the details of the economic system of centrally planned countries one would not easily understand these relations.

The head of the tax police was a pleasant, friendly man and a heavy consumer of *khat*. He told us that he would spend most afternoons in some club where he would chew *khat* while caressing some women who would be paid to keep the company of men. He swore that no sexual activities would take place. The caressing was not considered a sexual activity; it was just a form of companionship.

The tax police is an Italian institution that has influenced some other countries and especially transition countries. The Italian tax police, the *Guardia di Finanza*, are a large force of some 70,000. They report to the Minister of Finance, but are under the direct supervision of a general from the army. This army supervision is supposed to guarantee that this mini-army is not used for purposes different from those established by the law. In Italy this force has the responsibility, *inter alias*, of fighting drug smuggling, cigarette smuggling, tax evasion, money laundering, and other financial crimes. Normal crimes are dealt with by the *carabinieri*, another police force. The *Guardia di Finanza* audits taxpayers suspected of evading taxes and passes the information to the tax authorities for action. A frequent complaint, on the part of the *Guardia di Finanza*, is that the information that it passes on to the tax authorities often receives little follow up. Therefore, little of the presumably evaded taxes reported is ever recovered. When there is follow up, the procedures to recover the evaded taxes are very complex and can take years to reach a resolution. The reports, that the *Guardia di Finanza* prepares for the tax administration, are often challenged by the taxpayers. Special tax commissions are charged with deciding who is right. However these commissions are overworked and take years to reach decisions. The Italian government is currently (July 2010) trying to introduce a law that would require the taxpayers to make the payments up front, immediately after they are informed that they have evaded paying their taxes. Because mistakes are common, this is obviously a highly charged issue. It may be seen as punishment before being actually condemned.

The Italian model of tax police attracted a lot of attention on the part of governments of transition economies after the transition to democracy or to the market economy started. These governments saw this model as a way of employing productively the many individuals who had been employed by the countries' secret services. These security apparatuses had lost some of their justification after the transition. At one time or another countries such as Russia, China, Bulgaria and some others expressed strong interest in establishing an Italian-style tax police. In the Chinese case, the Fund even organized a seminar in Beijing to discuss the pros and cons of a tax police and hired an Italian expert on the matter to convince the Chinese *not* to follow the Italian example. In Somalia we had a hard time seeing any merit in having such a police.

In our work on the Somali tax system we were interested in estimating the share of total taxes into gross domestic product (GDP), the so-called tax burden. We were told that the official data available for GDP were not very good and that, recently, new estimates had been prepared by the national statistical office. Therefore, we visited the office and from its head we confirmed that in fact new estimations had been prepared. We asked for the new data and were surprised when we were told that they were state secrets and that only the President of Somalia, Mohamed Siad Barre, could authorize the release of the data. This reply reinforced a preoccupation that I have had over the years about politically-motivated manipulations of data and the relative indifference on the part of economists and even international institutions to this problem.

When one considers the campaign on the part of economists to make central banks independent from the government, one finds that no such attention or enthusiasm has gone into making statistical offices independent. In many cases these offices remain under the control of governments that, either directly or through the leverage of budgetary appropriations, can apply strong pressures on the officials of the statistical offices to massage or "revise," in a politically convenient direction, the data that are released. The problem of data manipulation or massaging extends beyond the National Statistical Offices because of the role that data play in many decisions.

Over the years I heard many times of cases where data had been manipulated. A minister of finance in Brazil, who incidentally was a very good man, had to resign from his position when he admitted, over what he thought was a switched off microphone, that the cost of living index was being manipulated so that the increase in wages and pensions that were indexed to the cost of living could be reduced. I wrote about this episode in one of my previous works, *The Charm of Latin America* (2010). In various countries, the Fund found out that the fiscal deficits reported by the governments within the context of Fund programs were lower than the actual deficits. In more recent years the European Commission discovered the same problem in connection with the fiscal deficits of some of its members. Greece got itself into great difficulties in 2010 when it was discovered that it had misreported its fiscal data in previous years. In recent years, there were also reports that the inflation data had been manipulated in Argentina.

In spite of this, there has been, over the years, only limited attention given to this problem. I recall my work on the underground economy around 1980. I thought that this work was important for the Fund because it raised questions in relation to statistics as central to Fund activities or Fund programs as national income. However, not only was there no interest, but a paper that I had written, on how to measure the underground economy, a paper that eventually became a widely cited and used paper, by economists all over the world, was turned down, for not dealing with an important topic, by the Fund's academic journal, the *IMF Staff Papers*. It was later published by an Italian journal, *Banca Nazionale del Lavoro Quarterly Review*, then a relatively important economic journal.

At the time of the writing of that paper Senator Robert Dole, one of the leaders of the Republican Party and a future presidential candidate, was holding hearings on the underground economy in the United States because this had become a hot topic. Because of my work on the topic, I was invited to appear before the Committee that he presided in Congress and to make a statement. As required, I asked for permission to do so from the Fund management, and all alarm bells started ringing. Somehow, there was little understanding that this was a problem of statistics and not of criminal activities. After a lot of internal discussion I was finally allowed to testify. However, for a long time, the Fund continued to show relatively little interest in the quality of the data or in the independence of statistical offices. Only in the 1990s did this problem attract some serious attention by the institution, especially after the 1997–98 financial crisis in Southeast Asia.

As part of our survey of the public finances of Somalia, we wanted to visit a municipality to learn about local finances. Our hosts arranged for us to visit Merka, an old town on the Red Sea from which, in earlier centuries, slaves had been shipped to various parts of the world. The town had old buildings and resembled the Mediterranean towns of North Africa. It had its own charm. Appointments had been made to visit the mayor and his assistants at the municipal building. The mayor, who was a dignified and courteous elderly gentleman, and two of his advisers, who were charged with the city finances, received us when we arrived. They seemed happy to receive a foreign delegation and must have felt important because of the visit. We listened to the litany of difficulties and learned about the various local fees and taxes that provided some income to the municipality. From the look of the place it was obvious that the tax revenue was very limited and that there was no money for many basic services or for the needed expenses for operation and maintenance. This lack of resources showed in the quality of the infrastructure. Here the presence of the state was not felt through its spending and taxing activities. While interested in some of the details we were not surprised by the general situation.

This conversation took place in the mayor's office in the old building of the municipality. While we were talking, a key that was dangling from the entrance door caught my attention. When we finished our meeting and we were ready to leave, I asked the mayor the age of the building and he replied that it was at least 200 years old. He then asked why I was interested in the building's age and I explained that I collected old keys and I had been intrigued by the key in his office that I assumed was as old as the building. Before leaving, we asked if there was any place in Merka where we could have lunch. He explained to our driver how to reach a particular restaurant and we left.

The "restaurant" turned out to be a semi-demolished building outside the city limits. It was an isolated building that we learned had been a small hotel where the Italians, during their occupation, would take their women. It had a little garden with a kind of pergola under which there were a few tables. It was very hot and there were lots of cats going all over the place. There was a grill on which they were roasting some chickens. This was the only food available with some bananas. This was another occasion where one could not have a weak stomach. One could either eat what was available or go hungry.

While we were attempting to eat, surrounded by cats and attacked by flies, we saw the mayor who, flanked by his two assistants, was coming towards us. In his hand he had a small package wrapped in paper and with a string around it. The mayor was wearing a broad smile. I got up to greet him and he told me that he had brought the key that I had noticed in his office. He explained that the door had not been locked for years so that the key did not serve any purpose. He said he would be happy if I accepted it as a souvenir of our visit to Merka. To say that I was truly touched by this act of kindness would be a great understatement. I tried to refuse it but he was insistent so that I accepted it thanking him and promising that I would place the key in a special section of my collection. He seemed to be happy that I would accept his gift.

We took another interesting trip out of Mogadishu. The authorities had arranged a trip to a collective farm about 100 kilometers from the capital. We went there by jeep because of the poor quality of the roads. In the jeep we had to carry a tank of gasoline because it would have been impossible to buy gasoline on the way and the jeep would need a refill of its tank. We were not happy to have the tank in the passenger section of the jeep, given the high temperature and the not insignificant risk of an accident on the road. But our escorts did not feel that there was any problem. Clearly assessment of risk is a relative concept; as income rises, risk becomes more concrete. The road to the village was very beautiful with interesting sights and occasional camel hordes. This part of Somalia was much greener than I had thought it would be. The village was by a river and was an experiment in communal life of which the government seemed to be quite proud. The Chinese or the Soviets must have been the advisor on this project. We saw children that looked healthy and happy. But we were told that the village was highly subsidized by the government. One problem for the village was the large number of crocodiles in the river that occasionally snapped some children. Apparently the crocodiles would lay immobile in the mud, at times for days, during which grass started growing on the mud that covered them. Occasionally someone, and especially children, would step on them with tragic consequences.

On the day of our departure, we went to the plane and sat in our assigned seats. Suddenly a delegation consisting of Mrs. Ali, Mrs. Hasha, and the Head of the Police arrived and came on board. They had brought us some gifts. Mine turned out to be a cleaned and embalmed lobster shell placed on a piece of wood! It was a strange gift, and I had no place to put it in. But it was a nice gesture again reflecting the developed sense of hospitality on the part of the Somali. I felt sorry and guilty when I had to leave the lobster in the plane.

During these trips I always felt the compulsion to buy something typical of the country. In Somalia there was practically nothing to buy. Some of my colleagues bought some shark teeth or shark jaws for their children. I bought a couple of very simple ivory bracelets which I placed in a small bag that I checked in the plane for Rome. When I got to my hotel in Rome I saw that the bag had been opened and the bracelets had disappeared. Their simplicity had not stopped the thief.

Before closing, I should mention that during the three weeks in Mogadishu we visited a few shops still run by Italians. These men had married Somali women during the Italian occupation before World War Two and had remained in Somalia. Some had never visited Italy again. The beauty of the Somali women must have been a major attraction.

When we returned to Washington, we wrote an extensive report that was sent to the authorities, but the economic and political situation kept deteriorating. I could never determine whether the report had any use in Mogadishu, although Fund economists from the geographical departments used it for their own reports. It is sad what happened to the country in the years that followed. Essentially the government disappeared and the standard of living kept going down. This was a transition toward chaos or toward a "failed state." In time the country almost proved that it could go on, with obvious difficulties, without a government. Almost 30 years later, the situation has not improved and it is difficult for me to relate the poor but superficially peaceful country that we saw in 1979 with the country described in newspaper articles and shown in movies such as *Black Hawk Down*. More recently Somali pirates have occupied the daily news with increasing frequency and have provided Somalia with a significant source of income. Terrorist groups have also moved into Somalia. This was not the kind of transition that the 1979 Fund mission had hoped would take place.

Chapter 11

Lebanon: Transition from Civil War

In May 2000, my wife and I arrived in Beirut at about 3 a.m. coming from Milan. My son's wife, Zena, is Lebanese. A friend of her family's was there to meet us when we arrived. He was an airport official and he rushed us through the immigration procedures and told us to wait by the baggage claims. We collected the bags, waited a while for the official, became impatient and decided to go through customs on our own. We did not have anything to declare. The customs officials were impressed by my red UN passport and let us go through without any checking. A red UN passport was given to staff members of international organizations above a certain rank and the UN was important in Lebanon. Individuals at lower rank had to travel with less impressive, blue passports that did not have such an announcement effect.

I had expected to see my son and his in-laws at the arrival but nobody was there. We waited for some time but nobody came. We were about to take a taxi to go to the hotel in Beirut where we had made reservations when my son, his wife, her father, and two drivers arrived. They had been given the wrong information about the plane's arrival time and had been waiting for much of the night at their place! After some hugging and kissing we drove to the Hotel in Beirut.

The Hotel Phoenicia had just reopened after extensive restoration and repairs. It had been badly damaged during the civil war and had been closed for several years. In the year 2000 Lebanon was still recovering from the civil war. Before the war, the Hotel Phoenicia had been the "Grand Hotel" of Beirut. Unfortunately for it, it was located near the "green line," the line that had separated the two warring sides during the long Lebanese Civil War. Most of the buildings in the area had been destroyed by what was a horrible conflict that lasted 15 years, until 1990, and killed some 150 thousand Lebanese. The ruins were still standing, or they had been cleared, leaving large empty spaces in the middle of the town. It was strange to see these empty areas in the middle of a crowded urban area. The Phoenicia was now again a grand, beautiful, five-star hotel. We climbed the red-carpeted, wide stairway and registered. When we got to the room we discovered that we had been given a room not facing the sea. We asked for a change and got the desired, but more expensive, room.

The next morning, I got up late and met an acquaintance, Mr. Suhail Karwa. Suhail, an economist, had worked for the IMF for many years before going back to Lebanon after the end of the civil war. While at the IMF, he had married a British girl who worked in my department. We met for lunch at a nice restaurant by the sea, a short, walking distance from the hotel. The customers in the restaurant looked expensively dressed, especially the women. The flight from Milan to Beirut had had a disproportionate number of beautiful female passengers, some with blond hair and long legs, who did not look Lebanese or Italian. I pointed this out to Suhail who explained that Beirut was a good place for "entertainers" from Eastern Europe. I could not help wondering what kind of entertainment they were engaged in but assumed that, in Lebanon, the entertainers from Eastern Europe met the rich customers from the Middle East in what must have been a mutually advantageous transaction. At the luncheon I got my first introduction to the poor Lebanese economy and the rich Lebanese cuisine, both highly interesting topics.

In the afternoon we visited my son, Vito Luigi, and my daughter-in-law, Zena, in their apartment. It was near the campus of the American University of Beirut (AUB) where my son was teaching. He has a Ph.D. in public health from the John Hopkins University and a Master in Economics from Boston University. His wife, Zena, has a medical degree from the United States and is the daughter of a Lebanese father and a German mother. Vito Luigi took us to see the campus of the American University, an impressive place overlooking the sea. The AUB has occupied a prominent role in the Middle East having trained many of its leaders over the decades. Remarkably it had remained open during the civil war even though it was near the green line! The AUB is a successful American institution that has managed to continue functioning, and to retain its prestige, even in the middle of the chaos brought about by the civil war and by other events. Its gates are guarded and it has a beautiful campus.

My son's apartment was close to Rafic Hariri's pharaonic mansion which could be seen from the apartment's terrace. Hariri, a self-made multibillionaire, had been the prime minister of Lebanon. He had made his fortune in Saudi Arabia and was admired by many people because he had financed thousands of Lebanese students studying abroad out of his own pockets. Lebanon has a highly educated and skilled population. While Hariri was prime minister, he launched a huge program of rebuilding and of public works hoping that tourists would soon return to his country. He was banking on the fact that, in the past, Lebanon had been compared to Switzerland and that Beirut was called the Paris of the Middle East. Unfortunately by 2000, the tourists had not yet come back in any significant numbers because of the political instability in the region. Partly as a consequence of the large rebuilding programs by Hariri, Lebanon ended up with a huge public debt and large fiscal deficits. In later years there would be significant increases in tourism, mostly from Arab countries, followed by falls after other bad events, such as the assassination of Prime Minister Hariri in 2005 and the Israel invasion in 2006. In the summers of 2003 and 2004 there were no hotel rooms available! Many of the tourists were from Arab countries. After September 11, 2001, tourists from Arab countries had felt less welcome in the United States and some had preferred the Lebanese destination for their vacations. In 2009 and 2010 tourism had again gone up sharply.

I had come to Lebanon to give an invited, public lecture and to discuss some economic issues with the new government and especially with Dr. Georges Corm, the Minister of Finance in the first, post-Hariri government. Dr. Corm had spent many years, during the long civil war, teaching in France. He had recently returned to Lebanon to join the new government. He was a charming man who reminded me of typical French intellectuals, highly educated and with slight leftist biases.

In the evening, my son's in-laws, Dr. and Mrs. Ghassan Hammoud, took us to a nice French restaurant called Le Rublau. It would rank high by international standards in terms of décor, quality of food, and service. Unfortunately, we were the only customers. We had a nice dinner and, afterward, we went back to the hotel and settled for a good night's sleep. I found my son's in-laws, whom I had only met once at my son's wedding in Washington, very charming. The father-in-law is a prominent physician and his wife is a pleasant, German lady. They had met in Germany when Dr. Hammoud was studying for his medical degree.

The next day, I prepared for my public lecture, which had been widely advertised in the media. The large lecture hall was full of prominent Lebanese and foreigners, including the Italian Ambassador, Dr. Giuseppe Cassini. My lecture, on the economic role of the state in the economy, a topic that had been interesting me for some time, went well and was followed by many questions.

Clearly this was a topic of particular interest to the Lebanese who, after the civil war were still debating what the role of the state should be in the Lebanese economy. The existence of very large public debt and fiscal deficit called for a modest spending role in future years. However, the many unmet needs of the country argued for a more extensive role. I had explained in my talk what the economic role of the state should be in a well-managed market economy. The problem is that many market economies are not well-managed. In this case does a country need more or less government? And is a country capable of financing a large role?

That night, the Finance Minister gave a dinner in my honor at the Hotel Sofitel. The dinner was attended by the governor of the Central Bank, several former ministers, the Italian ambassador, and other participants. From the Italian Ambassador I learned the origin of an Arabic expression frequently used in Lebanon that translates broadly as "it is the Italians' fault." This expression is used all the time by Lebanese. Thus, the Italians are blamed frequently for many things even bad weather! Apparently, during the First World War, an Italian battleship sank, by mistake, a Lebanese boat. It was clearly the Italians' fault! Thus, the expression entered the Lebanese Arabic language and it became part of it. Since then, when something does not go well, it is always the Italians' fault! This, however, has not prevented Italy from becoming Lebanon's main trading partner and from developing a friendly relation with the country. After the 2006 war, it was Italian soldiers that manned the UN outposts. They were generally welcome by the Lebanese.

My wife and I made arrangements with the hotel travel office to go to Baálbek, the grandiose Roman temple, on the following morning. The cost of the trip, which included lunch, was highly reasonable. In the morning we met the driver and a female guide. There were no other people in the group. The guide was a pleasant, young, and well-educated woman, who spoke good English. We left the city and progressively made our way toward the mountains. Given the reputation of these mountains and especially of the Bekaa (or Beqaa) Valley, acquired during the civil war and expanded in American movies and television programs, we were unavoidably nervous. The road was crowded and every few kilometers there was a checkpoint. In 2000 the Syrians had a continued presence in Lebanon but in a discrete way. We had been told that nothing important happened in Lebanon without their approval or knowledge. Along the way, we learned to distinguish Lebanese from

Syrian checkpoints. At each checkpoint the car slowed down but it was never asked to stop.

The car made its way up the mountains and I enjoyed the scenery. Being springtime there was green all around us and many flowers. Lebanon is famous for having beautiful mountains and very fertile areas for agriculture. I was surprised by the amount of destruction still visible along the road, ten years after the end of the civil war. Many of the houses or buildings along the way had been badly damaged or destroyed and had not been rebuilt or repaired. The civil war must have been terrible, and its effects were not limited to one area. Along the road there were lots of pictures of President Assad of Syria and of the head of the Hezbollah, Sheikh Hassan Nasrallah. By coincidence this trip was taking place the day after the Israelis had suddenly withdrawn from the south of Lebanon, which they had occupied for many years after the 1982 invasion, so that there was a lot of visible excitement along the roads.

Once we got over the mountains, we had a view of the Bekaa Valley and we started our descent. The valley was very green, and looked fertile and peaceful. It was hard to believe that this peaceful and beautiful place had seen many atrocities in past years. As we approached the city of Baálbek, we ran into hundreds of people crowding the streets and carrying flags, loudspeakers, and even guns. They did not look threatening, and our escorts did not seem concerned, but we were inevitably apprehensive. Some people were collecting money for the Hezbollah. Some came to our car, and the guide gave them some money. She told us that with the money collected, the Hezbollah, a Shiite organization, supported by Iran and Syria, and classified by the American government as a terrorist organization, ran hospitals and charity programs, in addition to occasionally fighting Israel. The guide asked someone what was happening and was told that a man from Baálbek, who had been a prisoner of the Israeli for 17 years, had been released the night before and today he was returning home, to what remained of his family. During the time he had been a prisoner, his father had died. The crowd was a welcome-home parade.

We finally reached the entrance to the ruins of Baálbek, bought tickets and went inside the temple. I was not ready for the magnificent spectacle that the ruins present. They are among the most magnificent Roman ruins I have seen anywhere. It was strange that the Romans had built something of this size and splendor in this now isolated place. Baálbek must have had a great strategic or symbolic importance in ancient times. In size Baálbek almost reminded me of Luxor in Egypt. It is also extraordinary because of the quality of the stone carvings. Many of the immense stones and the huge columns that one time must have supported the roof of the temple were beautifully carved with faces of gods, lions, flowers and other symbols. A mystery is how the huge stones were carried to this place.

We were the only visitors in the large area inside the temple, and while we were taking photos in total isolation we could hear guns being fired nearby. We hoped that the shots reflected gestures of joy and that the guns were being fired in the air and not at somebody. Nonetheless, we were a bit concerned. Because the temple does not have any covering now, I also could not help wonder what happens to the bullets when guns are fired in the air. They must return to earth. What if they land on someone's head, including mine? This is the kind of question that I would have liked to ask a scientist. We assumed and hoped that the firing announced the arrival of the freed prisoner.

I would have liked to spend much more time at the temple and to take a larger number of photos. I marveled at the huge columns that must have sustained a high roof and at lions and other animal portraits in the carvings or the stones. The weather was splendid, and the sun was shining in a cloudless sky, but it was not hot. It was a most pleasant visit. I concluded that Baálbek alone was worth a visit to Lebanon.

When we came out of the temple, there were crowds in the streets. We came to a corner where there was a large concentration of people. I noticed that on the sidewalk there was a lot of blood. I feared that someone had been shot but then I saw that the blood was coming from a dead sheep. The guide said that the sheep had been sacrificed to God, to thank God for the return of the native son. She also told us that the meat of the sheep would be donated to an orphanage. I learned that orphanages are common in the Middle East because children that do not have immediate families are rarely adopted by strangers. Because of religions considerations they are not available for adoption by individuals who are not Muslim, and within families there are no unwanted children.

We stopped for lunch at a restaurant, in an old hotel, in the town of Baálbek, and were served a truly spectacular Lebanese lunch with lots of servings and friendly waiters. This was the lunch included in the modest price of the tour. The waiters were very pleasant and we were the only visitors in the restaurant. They told us that, before the civil war, world-famous people had stayed at this hotel. After lunch we stopped at a place where, we were told, some of the best wines of Lebanon have been made for centuries. I am not sure about its name but I believe that it was Ksara. The wine is stored in caves hundreds of meters long built by the Romans two thousands years ago! We were taken for a visit of the caves and bought a few bottles of white wine. I was a bit surprised to see wine production in Lebanon but then I reminded myself that this was not a fully Muslim country. In any case Algeria, a Muslim country, has recently started to produce again the good wine that it had produced during the French colonial period. After this visit we made our way back to Beirut. There was a lot of traffic on the road but it moved fast so that we got back to the hotel at a decent time.

The next day we went to Sidon to visit the family of my daughter-in-law. On the way to Sidon we passed by the site of the old American embassy where hundreds of marines were killed in a horrible truck bombing in 1983. This had happened during the, earlier, invasion of Lebanon by the Israeli army, to stop the activities against Israel of the Palestinians who had been pushed out of Israel in 1948 and had established a kind of mini state in a part of Lebanon. The 1982 Israeli invasion had led to some atrocious episodes of cruelty, some of which are described in a recent Israeli film, *Waltz with Bashir*. This movie reports on the massacre by Lebanese Christians against unarmed Palestinians at the camps of Sabra and Shatila, a massacre that was not stopped by the Israeli forces that were aware of it. At that time Ariel Sharon was Israel defense minister. Another Israeli film, *Lebanon*, has also reported on the 1982 war and has won the Gold Lion as the best foreign language movie at the Venice Festival. The bombing of the American Embassy prompted President Reagan to withdraw the American troops from Lebanon. We passed by an area where Palestinian refugees have occupied some land and have built poor shacks or shops. We had the impression of being in a different country. This area looked much poorer and different from the rest of Lebanon. We crossed various checkpoints without being stopped and passed by one of the Palestinian camps.

The Palestinians here are in a limbo that will continue to contribute to the instability of Lebanon and the area. They moved into Lebanon in large numbers during the Arab-Israeli War in 1948, when Israel was created. They cannot get citizenship status in Lebanon because their large number (about 400 thousands) would upset the delicate Lebanese balance between Christians and Muslims, a balance based on the assumption that the population of Lebanon (officially about 4 million) is half Christian and half Muslim. The existing political arrangements are based on this assumption. Adding to the total population some ten percent of mostly Muslim people would make the Christians a clear minority and transform Lebanon into a Muslim country. There has been no official census taken in Lebanon since 1932 to challenge the assumption of equality between the two sides. This assumed balance is the rationale for the division of political power codified in the Lebanese constitution. That balance helps keep the country from precipitating again into a civil war.

The existing political arrangement is that the President must be a Maronite Christian, the Prime Minister a Sunni Muslim, and the Speaker of Parliament a Shia Muslim. How delicate the political balance is could be seen by the fact that when in 2004 the government was pressured to resume capital punishment (after a five year hiatus) for a Shiite Muslim guilty of having killed eight people, it felt compelled to execute one Christian convict and one Sunni Muslim. The three were executed simultaneously in a sign of equality before the law, as reported in *The New York Times, International.* It is not clear what will happen to the Palestinians who live in Lebanon over the long run. They cannot go back to the places where they came from, now Israel, and cannot become full citizens in Lebanon. Because of their limited opportunities, including the legal prohibition to engage in many activities, their income is very low, even by Lebanese standards, and is likely to remain so.

We reached Sidon and were received by Dr. Hammoud, my son's father-in-law. Dr. Hammoud is a proud and distinguished-looking gentleman. He was happy to show us the modern hospital that he built and owns. My daughter-in-law, Zena, works there. My son contributes to the running of the hospital in addition to his teaching occupation. The hospital has about 350 beds, and more than 1,000 people work in it, making it the largest employer in the South of Lebanon. I was much surprised by how modern and how clean it was. This hospital had performed the first heart transplant in the Middle East, outside of Israel. It is used by one of the universities as a teaching hospital and by the UN personnel in Lebanon. Dr. Hammoud was obviously an important man in Sidon, and everyone seemed to know and respect him. A gynecologist by training, he has delivered some 25,000 babies in the area. By now some of these babies have grown to occupy important positions. The hospital remained open during the civil war, in spite of the danger and the difficulties. Dr. Hammoud told me that both Arafat and Sharon had visited it at some point. The hospital also played an important role during the 2006 conflict with Israel. The street where the hospital is located has been named after Dr. Hammoud.

We visited the town of Sidon (or Saida), one of the oldest cities in the world. There is historical evidence that it already existed 5,000 years ago! It is exceeded in age by another Lebanese City, Byblos, an ancient port that already existed 7,000 years ago. Sidon has seen a lot of history. It is here that Alexander the Great won one of his major battles. He encountered fierce resistance from the defenders of the city and after his victory had 3000 of those who had resisted him crucified. We visited the old part of the town, which seemed to come straight out of the Middle Ages, with very narrow streets that form a kind of labyrinth. Dr. Hammoud was greeted and welcomed everywhere we went. I indulged in my photographic hobby and many small children seemed happy to pose for me. In one corner, by a small coffee shop, there were about ten elderly men all seated and all smoking water pipes (*arhgileh*). It was a scene straight from the past. I wanted to take a picture but I hesitated until Dr. Hammoud told me that it was okay to do so. We also visited various old shops where the tools used were still those used centuries ago.

We went for lunch at a fish restaurant by the sea (Saida Rest House). It is in front of an old fortress, or castle, built by the Crusaders in the 11th century. Unfortunately the fortress was closed so that we could not visit the inside of it. We had a nice meal based on fish, and my wife, Maria, a non-smoker, tried the hubble-bubble (the water pipe). She said that she enjoyed it. When we returned to Beirut in the late afternoon we were stopped at one of the checkpoints. This was the only time we were stopped during our visit. It was dark and I could not tell whether it was a Syrian or a Lebanese checkpoint. After checking the driver's documents we were waved on.

Over the next couple of days, I spent much time with the experts at the Ministry of Finance. We discussed the fiscal situation that seemed disastrous: the public debt was about 140 percent of GDP; the fiscal deficit was 16–17 percent of GDP; and the taxes collected barely covered the interest payments on the public debt. At that time my department at the IMF was assisting Lebanon with the introduction of a Value Added Tax. This would provide the new government with some badly-needed public revenue. An Egyptian expert, Abdel Rahman, had been involved in this project, and his work was producing good results. The senior staff of the Ministry hoped that they would also be able to raise some revenue from the sale of public enterprises. They complained that a kind of cartel of banks was keeping interest rates higher than they needed to be and asked me to convey to the Fund a request to look into this matter. This was another example of the natural debate between central banks and ministries of finance about the desirable level of the interest rate.

On the Sunday we visited Sidon again. We were met by an ex-mayor of Sidon who first invited us to his splendid house for breakfast and then he took us to see the ruins of Tyre (*Sour*), a large, antique Roman city by the sea. It is much larger than Baálbek but less spectacular, though it is still a striking place. Tyre was important because it was the place where traders set out to go to the Silk Road to trade their wares with the Chinese. Thus it was an important point on the contacts between the Roman World and the Chinese World. I discovered that the ex-mayor was related to the urologist I went to in Washington! I have always been surprised how often it happens that in a world with some six billion people I occasionally run into strangers, often in far away places, and discover that we have common acquaintances. In 2006 Tyre was much damaged in the Israeli invasion of Lebanon.

We went for lunch at the rural house of the Hammouds. The house is made of white stones that glitter in the sun. The location, up the mountains and overlooking the sea, is very beautiful. It is surrounded by 70 hectares of fruit trees, including all the fruits that grow around the Mediterranean Seas, including bananas. It seems like the Garden of Eden and provides visual evidence why Lebanon is such an attractive place.

In the evening, we went to a hotel for a wedding party for one of Zena's cousins. The bride was marrying someone who had made a lot of money in Saudi Arabia. Saudi Arabia seems to be the Eldorado for clever Lebanese. There was dancing, much entertainment and a lot of drinking. This was not the Middle East that one sees on TV programs. At the party I saw some of the miniest mini-skirts and lowest plunging necklines I have ever seen. In fact this struck me about Lebanon: the contrast between the ultra-modern and ultra-daring, on one side, and the conservative Muslim attires, worn by others. I was told that the Iranian government was actually paying a stipend to Lebanese women who agreed to wear the *chador*.

I went back to Lebanon in 2002 for a brief visit to see my son and his family. At that time Hariri was again Prime Minister, and the economic future of Lebanon looked much more promising than in 2000. The center of Beirut had been completely transformed in the last two years and looked again modern and beautiful. Many rich Arabs had been buying some of the beautiful, newly-built apartments. The signs of destruction from the past civil war had largely disappeared and elegant restaurants and shops had opened. Tourists had returned in large numbers. The future of Lebanon again looked good and the country seemed to be on the way to reacquire its title of Switzerland of the Middle East. However, the conflicts that had led to the civil war were still there and some were growing in intensity. In February 2005 there was the horrible assassination of Hariri and, the next year, the new Israeli invasion of Lebanon, following the kidnapping and killing of some Israeli soldiers by Hezbollah forces. The Israeli invasion created a lot of new destruction, killed many people, and destroyed a lot of infrastructure. Uncertainly about the future returned, together with several bombings that killed individuals that had been critical of the Syrian role in Lebanon.

The assassination of Prime Minister Hariri, and the Lebanese and international reactions to it, led to the end of the quasi-occupation of Lebanon by Syria. In the period after 2006 Lebanon largely recovered from the effects of the assassination and of the Israeli invasion showing again the remarkable resiliency of the population. The fact that there are some 12 million Lebanese throughout the world, who continue to send money to their relatives in Lebanon, helps a lot. Calm has returned, and the economy withstood well the 2008–2009 financial crisis. The Lebanese banks showed great ability to avoid the crisis and to deal with some of its effects. The Hezbollah are now part of the government. Lebanese artists have been doing well in the international art scene. Even Lebanese fashion is doing well. In 2010 a young lady of Lebanese descent became the U.S. beauty queen. It is difficult to predict what the future will bring. For the time being the economy is growing at one of the fastest rates in the world. As a Lebanese-born financial writer, Nassim Nicholas Taleb, wrote in one of his books, randomness plays a larger role in history than people realize. The internal divisions are still there. And the tension with Israel remains and occasionally leads to difficulties. The Palestinians are still living in great numbers in Lebanon. And its public debt is still one of the highest among countries. Otherwise all is (relatively) quiet on the Lebanese front.

Chapter 12

Morocco: Transition from Colonialism and from Overregulation

Between 1978 and the late 1990s I visited Morocco several times for different reasons: to provide technical assistance to the authorities; to attend and speak at conferences; or simply to discuss policy issues with government officials. I dealt with different ministers of finance and with a changing cast of government officials. I always found the experience interesting and the country fascinating. During the earlier visits the country was still adjusting its institutions and policies from the time it had been under a French protectorate (1912 to 1956) to one with a constitutional monarchy but with a lively political opposition. As a French protectorate the country had been over-regulated. In the more recent years it had tried to reduce the regulatory constraints.

I remember well my first visit there in 1978, when the Moroccan government asked the IMF for assistance to make its tax system less dependent on import duties. In this visit to Rabat, a young and able Moroccan, Mr. Ben Brick, was assigned to accompany me during the visit. He would become the Moroccan Director of Taxation in later years. I spent a few days familiarizing myself with the Moroccan tax system and learning about its strength and peculiarities. At that time the tax system was not guided by any well-defined tax principle. Rather, it seemed to be guided by the "cynical law of taxation": grab the revenue wherever you can! If there was an implicit principle followed, probably inherited from the days when Morocco was a French protectorate, it was that of providing maximum protection, through the use of high import duties, to domestic production. By discouraging imports, a high enough import duty allows domestic producers to continue producing, even when the costs of production are much higher than those of potential foreign competitors. This implies that the country allocates excessive national resources for the production of products that could be imported more cheaply in terms of the use of domestic resources.

At the end of the mission, I wrote a report trying to explain that if the government wanted to tax consumption, it could do it better with domestic sales taxes. These would not distinguish between domestic and imported products. Import duties should have the objective of providing *intentional* protection to the domestic production of specific products and should not be used to satisfy revenue objectives and thus, at the same time, providing *un*intentional protection to domestic producers. The report was written for the benefit of the minister of finance.

During my stay in Rabat I met the Minister of Trade and Industry and explained to him the fundamental recommendation of the report. He saw the problem from a different angle. He defended the use of import duties for providing protection to domestic producers. He saw this as his main objective. I asked him what he thought should be a reasonable level of protection, as measured by the level of import duties. He gave me a puzzled look and replied that he gave a producer the protection that he needed. I asked him, rhetorically, whether 50 percent would be enough. He repeated that he would give whatever would be necessary. I asked him whether 100 percent or 1000 percent would be acceptable to him. He kept repeating that his policy was very simple: to give the enterprises *whatever* level of protection they needed to continue producing domestically. The world was very simple as far as this minister was concerned. Unfortunately, during my many years as an economic adviser, I met many ministers for whom the world was that simple.

I returned a few months later with a full mission that included a Belgian colleague, Luc De Wulf, with whom I had worked in Portugal, and Peter Griffith, an expert in tax administration, who had a law degree from Harvard. We wrote a report that became a reference point for future tax reforms in Morocco and that tried to introduce specific economic principles or criteria in the use of tax instruments. The reforms progressively separated the protective use of import duties from the revenue use of taxes on consumption. Over the years, in part because of agreements between Morocco and the European Union, revenue from import duties fell significantly and revenue from value added taxes and excises increased significantly.

At the time of this mission, the Director of Customs was a politically powerful man. He was politically more powerful than the Minister of Finance. I recall some events that indicate just how powerful he was. When the King became convinced that a tax reform was necessary, he made a public announcement in which he stated that the tax reform would be made by the Director of Customs *and* by the Minister of Finance. The order in which the two individuals were mentioned was indicative of their respective power. Their personal offices also reflected their powers. The Director of Customs had a huge office in Casablanca, full of archeological pieces and beautiful furniture. The Minister of Finance had a much more modest office in Rabat. While the Director of Customs had a large, expensive, chauffer-driven limousine, the Minister had a more modest vehicle.

The day when the mission was to leave Morocco the Director of Customs asked us to meet him in his office in Casablanca to explain the content of the report. We put our suitcases in our cars in Rabat and went to the Director's office from where we would drive to the international airport which was also in Casablanca. The Director showed great interest in our report and we had a lengthy discussion on some of its points. He realized that the recommended reform would reduce import tax revenue and, thus, indirectly, his power. The discussion was taking longer than anticipated and we were getting a bit nervous because our departure time was getting close. Each time I mentioned that we had to be on the way, the Director said not to worry. I became progressively more concerned that we would miss our flight. At one point, the Director assured us that the plane would not leave without his orders. Finally, the meeting ended and we were taken by car, with police escort and with sirens blaring, directly to the door of the plane that was waiting for us with its engines already running. We never went through passport controls and airport inspection. Our check-in had been done automatically by the assistants of the Director. But those were the days before terrorism became a major concern. The only other time when I had a similar experience was in Burkina Faso during a meeting with President Blaise Campaoré, attended also by Alassane Ouattara, a former colleague at the Fund who became President of the Central Bank of West African countries and Prime Minister of the Ivory Coast. But in this case the power was in the hand of the President of a country.

At the time of this mission there were a lot of rumors about corruption in the Moroccan customs. This issue would retain much interest in years to come and at a later time the IMF would be asked to assist in dealing with this problem. We were somewhat surprised that many of the senior officials in Customs with whom we had contacts were driving expensive Mercedes cars in a country where government salaries were very low and import duties on these cars were very high. When I commented on this to one of the assistants of the Director of Customs, he simply answered, straight-faced, that the Rabat–Casablanca road was a dangerous one so that a strong and reliable car was needed! There was a joke that circulated at the time about the exam that had to be taken in Morocco to get a job in Customs. The story went that the day of the test, the first candidate went in, was asked a question and failed the test. The second candidate met the same fate. But then the third went in and passed. The other candidates asked him what question he has been asked; he replied that he had been asked to conjugate the verb "to take." His answer had been: I take, you take; you take, I take; I take, you take . . . This question of corruption at customs engaged the Fiscal Affairs Department of the Fund in technical assistance aimed at eliminating some discretion on the part of customs officials and introducing better controls on their actions.

During the three weeks of the Fund mission in Morocco we had innumerable meetings with employees in the Ministry of Finance and in Customs but also tried to see a bit of the country. We were staying in Rabat at the Hilton Hotel, a hotel somewhat rundown at the time but with a large and beautiful garden that allowed one to take walks in the garden without having to go out of the hotel. One night we decided to experience a typical Moroccan dinner, because we were tired of eating the same international fare at the hotel restaurant. We asked the concierge of the hotel for advice on where to go and he told us that on the roof of one of the other hotels there was a restaurant that was an exact replica of a Bedouin tent. It also served genuine Moroccan cuisine and had Moroccan entertainment. He advised us to make reservations and to go early so that we could get good seats.

We made reservations and went to this restaurant. In the tent-restaurant there were cushions on the floor on which guests sat. When we arrived, the place was empty so that we could choose where to sit. Bit by bit the tent filled up and we ordered our food. Like most Moroccan food, it was very tasty but it had to be eaten with our hands, which was a bit unsettling. After the dinner came the entertainment. An announcer informed the clients that this was a special night and that, accordingly, the entertainment would be special and unusual. He announced that there would be a Japanese female singer, who was a friend of one of the Moroccan princesses, who would sing for the guests. This was the first surprise. The second was that the Japanese singer would sing Argentine tangos. Thus for our typical Moroccan night, we ended up listening to a Japanese singer, singing Argentine tangos in a Bedouin tent! I remembered this episode especially years later when one of my colleagues at the IMF, Carlos Silvani, an Argentine who had been Director of Taxation in Argentina, wanted to learn to dance the tango with his Argentine wife in Washington. They took tango dancing lessons from a very good teacher. However, the tango teacher was a Russian émigré who had never been to Argentina and who did not speak a word of Spanish. This was another of the many peculiar manifestations of globalization.

We were in Rabat during the "fête du mouton" when families buy a live sheep, which may weigh more than two hundred pounds, kill it, following a very precise protocol imposed by religion, and spend the following two to three days eating as much meat as they can. At the time of the mission few Moroccan families had refrigerators so that the meat could not be kept more than a couple of days. I took a picture of a donkey carrying a tied, live sheep on its back that won an honorable mention at the Bank-Fund annual photo exhibition. The members of the mission were invited to the dinner by our driver and enjoyed a very nice serving of mutton cooked slowly with eggs in a clay pot in the oven. It was delicious and we much appreciated the invitation. The driver considered it a great honor to have us in his modest house. In a sign of how more culturally liberal Morocco was compared to, say, Saudi Arabia, the wife of the driver was with us during the dinner. In a similar situation in Saudi Arabia, the lady of the house had never appeared.

At the end of the mission, we were taken to that extraordinary city that is Fez. On the way to Fez, the driver would stop at various mosques to pray for a few minutes and we would wait in the car. At one stop I moved close to the entrance of the mosque but I was politely told by someone that non-Muslims were not allowed to enter. This contrasted with experiences in Turkey and Egypt where I was invited or even encouraged to enter into the mosques. This shows that the Muslim world is as fragmented as the Christian world.

Fez is a city straight out of the Middle Ages. The old part has streets that are so narrow that when a small cart, normally pulled by a donkey, comes down the street one has to move inside one of the shops that line the street, because there is not enough space for both. The shops are also incredibly small, often no larger than 40 square feet but are packed with all kinds of merchandises. During another, later visit to Fez in which I was accompanied by the head of the tax office of Fez, I was told that the taxation of the small shops followed the principle of *forfeit*, that is, the taxable base was assessed on the basis of the square footage of the shop. The larger the square footage, the higher the presumed taxable base, and thus the higher the tax. The tax created a strong incentive to utilize the space to the maximum. This approach dispensed with the need for tax accountants or for keeping records.

Morocco is famous for its leather goods. In France, "Maroquinerie" is still the name for a shop that sells leather goods. We visited a tannery in which leather was processed in the same way as it had been centuries earlier. One felt sorry for the workers who worked there and who were directly exposed to the chemicals used in the tanning. We wondered what their life expectancy was.

The old part of Fez gives one the impression of stepping back to the 12th or 13th century. Apart from the width of the streets and the labyrinth that they form, a visitor is struck by the variety of unusual shops. For example, we passed by a "hotel" used by people who brought goods from the countryside. At that time the cost of lodging in this hotel was U.S. 70 cents per night. This cost also included the place for the donkey that often accompanied the peasant! In Fez there is perhaps the oldest university in the world, older than Bologna, which is over 900 years old. In the Middle Ages, Christian monks from European countries would hide their identity and come to Fez to acquire the more advanced knowledge, in mathematics, astronomy, and philosophy that was available in Fez. It was a kind of early version of intellectual espionage.

In March 1988 I went back to Morocco to attend a conference in the town of Mohammedia. The Ministry of Finance of Morocco and the IMF had jointly organized the conference. The World Bank also participated. The theme was "Economic Policy for Growth in Developing Countries." Mr. Mohammed Berrada, then the Finance Minister of Morocco, opened the event. The debate was lively and a book was published in Morocco with the papers presented at the conference and some of the comments. The Fund was criticized for enforcing standardized adjustment programs on countries. In response to this criticism I commented that Fund programs were like girls. They all look the same at a great distance but the closer you get to them, the more you appreciate the differences in their looks.

At the end of the conference, the staff of the ministry had organized a driving tour for my wife and me so that we could see other cities, such as Meknes and Fez, and we could also admire the beautiful countryside during early spring, when it is very green. I recall that the morning when we left Mohammedia it was very foggy and the visibility was limited to few feet. The car had to travel on a two lane road with traffic going in both directions. In spite of the limited visibility, our driver was going fast and was surpassing the cars in front of us. To do so he had to use the lane for the incoming traffic. Because of the fog he could not see if there were incoming vehicles. I had to tell him several times to slow down and not to attempt passing because he was risking his and our lives. Somehow I had the impression that my evaluation of the risk was different from his. Perhaps he believed in destiny while I believed that our actions play a role in outcomes.

Once the fog cleared and the sun came out, we could admire the splendid fields, some all green and some covered with flowers. We passed by several mosques and by several impressive palaces. We were told that some of these palaces belonged to the king. I could not figure out why the king needed so many palaces but then I realized that kings need to travel and when they travel they cannot go to hotels where common mortals go. Thus, their need for many palaces. I admired the imposing walls that protected some of the cities. Many Moroccan cities still have a limited numbers of entrances through doors in the city walls. I still recall the view of Fez seen from the hills around it, while we were approaching it.

During this second visit to Fez, the local director of taxation met us and took us around the old part of the city providing explanations and answers to some of my questions. He was accompanied by his 16-year old daughter and both spoke English. He was obviously well known by all the merchants who greeted him with great respect and cordiality. We passed by a shop that sold handmade, Moroccan carpets. Moroccan carpets have their own style and are somewhat different from those of Iran, Turkey, Pakistan or other countries in the Middle East. They are, thus, different from the ones we normally consider oriental carpets. The director invited me to go into the shop and take a look at the carpets. I told him that I did not need any carpets but he stressed that there was no obligation to buy any. So we went into the shop. In spite of the modest appearance from the outside, the inside of the shop was that of a beautiful, large mansion. The house was very large and had rooms in upper floors that, in traditional Arab houses, were reserved for the women. There were thousands of carpets all over the place.

The owner of the shop came to greet us and showed great cordiality vis-à-vis the tax director. Because it was almost one o'clock, he invited us for lunch that, he insisted, would be simple and informal.

Before I could express an opinion, we were taken to a terrace, covered by a pergola, on the roof of the house. Here we were served a marvelous lunch which started with *pastilla* and continued with *poulet au citron*—chicken marinated in lemon juice. It was served with the juice of pomegranates, the first time I had seen this juice, and with the ever-present *thé à la menthe*. Pomegranate juice has now become available in the United States and is advertised as being rich in antioxidants. Its popularity has been growing in recent years.

When the lunch was over, we went downstairs and various carpets were shown to me. Considering that I did not have any need for, or any intention to buy carpets, I left the shop with the equivalent of about $3,000 of goods. After such a marvelous lunch, I would have felt bad not to buy anything. These are the little "traps" that at times reduce our freedom of action. Experimental economics has, in recent years, identified some of these traps. When I was paying for the carpets, the owner of the shop casually suggested, in the presence of the tax director, that it would be better if the receipt that he gave me for the purchase showed only a $500 purchase so that I would not have any problems with customs at my arrival in the United States. Of course, he never mentioned that the same receipt would, I presume, determine his tax liability in Morocco. The director of taxation did not seem to find anything strange about this faking of the invoice.

When I returned to Washington I found out that the owner of the shop was the cousin of a colleague of mine at the Fund, who was the representative of Morocco at the Fund Board of Executive Directors. He would later become the President of the African Development Bank. By coincidence a few days after my return to Washington there was a long article in the travel section of the *New York Times* on Moroccan carpets. There were pictures of the shop where I had done my purchases.

We were also taken to Marrakesh where we spent the night at the famous hotel Mamounia which belonged to the Moroccan Railroad. The hotel is just extraordinary with rooms that reflect the most refined taste of Islamic décor and art. It has also a beautiful garden and a large swimming pool by which a very rich assortment of food is served so that one has the choice of having lunch by the pool. This hotel is much frequented by rich French tourists. The French women generally went in the pool, or sat by it for lunch, wearing nothing more than the lower part of their tiny bikinis. I could not help wondering about the impact that the sight of these practically-naked women had on the Moroccan workers who served them or assisted them by the pool. These workers would go home and find their women covered from head to toe. How would an orthodox Muslim react to these scenes? Is this one way in which Western culture has given rise to fundamentalist reactions? I could not help but wonder.

Marrakesh is a very interesting and exotic city. It is the place where Africa truly meets Europe. In this sense it is different from Rabat or Fez, which are typical Arab cities, or from Casablanca, which, in spite of being on the Atlantic, is culturally a Mediterranean city. In Marrakesh the presence and the influence of Africa is much more noticeable. The city has marvelous palaces, mosques and monuments. Being close to high mountains it also gives tourists the choice of going to the mountain or to the sea within a short period of time. In this sense it is like Beirut. Its squares show many unusual spectacles, some including snakes, monkeys, or acrobats.

During these trips to Morocco I started a collection of old keys. The Moroccan keys were the first I bought after having seen some old keys hanging on the whitewashed walls of a French coffee shop during a trip to the countryside of Southern France in the early 1970s. Key collecting became a strong interest for me and over the years I managed to get together a fairly good and extensive collection. I have learned more and more about keys and, eventually, about locks, and acquired several books on them. I also discovered that there are museums dedicated to keys and locks, such as the museum Bricard in Paris, in the same square as the Picasso Museum. It has a beautiful collection of old keys and locks. I also found out that many people collect them. The ones that I bought in Morocco were the ones that started my collection.

At the beginning of my key collecting I noticed that this market was very inefficient so that relatively similar keys could cost in one place as much as ten times as in other places. As time passed, I noticed that the law of one price was slowly asserting itself so that prices began to converge. This was evidence that more exchanges were taking place. But of course because each key is, in some way, unique, combined with the fact that there is still little information available to the collector, and no formal place where trading occurs, means that prices can still be very different from place to place. Over the years I made a point of visiting markets or shops where I could find old keys or locks. I did this during the three months I spent in Budapest in 1997. I made particularly good buys in China and in my earlier trips to Russia. In both cases I bought locks rather than keys. I found the price of keys very expensive in shops in Rome.

In June 1996, I returned to Morocco at the request of the Minister of Finance, accompanied by two colleagues, George Abed and Christopher Grandcolas. George Abed, a Palestinian with a Jordanian passport, would later become president of the Central Bank of Palestine. Christopher Grancolas was a French expert in tax administration. Ben Brick, the young man who had accompanied me in my first visit almost 20 years earlier, met us at the airport. By this time he was the Director of Taxation of Morocco.

I had come to Morocco at the insistent invitation of the Minister of Finance. He wanted us to look at the tax system and at customs to tell him if these institutions had major management problems. The year before, a high-level French team had studied these institutions and had prepared a scathing report on the Customs Administration. In recent months the Customs Administration had been accused of permitting contraband and of facilitating the smuggling of illegal drugs. This had become big business, and the King had intervened. The Director of Customs was arrested and some rich Moroccans were found guilty. The Minister of Finance was having political difficulties because the accused head of customs was a close friend of his and he had appointed him. At this stage, it was not yet clear to me what was expected from the Fund mission. By coincidence Luc De Wulf, who was now working for the World Bank, was also visiting Morocco. He had been part of the 1978 mission.

We had gone to the Hyatt Hotel, the same hotel I had stayed before when it had been a Hilton Hotel. The hotel had been upgraded and renamed. It was much nicer than it had been earlier and the garden at the back was more magnificent than 20 years earlier. However, there was far more construction around it than in the earlier years. The weather was splendid and, on arrival, I had my first *thé à la menthe*! In the evening, Ben Brick came to get us and invited us to a restaurant called *Le Entrecote*. It was a lovely restaurant and we had a very good fish dinner while we discussed fiscal developments in Morocco.

The next morning I got up early so that I could take a brisk walk in the garden. Later, Luc De Wulf called and we agreed to meet for dinner in the evening. We were supposed to meet the Minister at 10:00 that morning but the meeting was postponed to the next day. We had a long meeting with the senior staff of the Direction des Impots. Some of the staff had already been there 18 years earlier and were happy to see us. However, the problems in the tax system had not disappeared. There was a lot of pressure for preferential tax treatment and for lower rates for both income taxes and value added taxes. The Director of Taxation was often faced with strong political pressures that he could not avoid or always resist.

In the afternoon we had a long meeting with the head of the Moroccan Treasury. The Treasury is responsible for receiving tax payments and for meeting authorized public expenditures. We discussed tax arrears and what they did about them, how they contacted taxpayers who had not made payments on time, and how the Treasury managed its cash. Morocco had a French-influenced system that is different from that found in Anglo-Saxon countries where the tax payments are made directly to the tax administration. The French system separates the responsibility for the determination of tax liability from that related to the collection of tax payments. As a consequence, compliance costs as well as administrative costs tend to be higher.

We ended the day by visiting the data center at the Ministry. There had been a major revolution since I had first come to Morocco. Now state-of-the-art computer technology allowed the retrieval and the manipulation of an amazing amount of statistical information. It was possible to retrieve information on (a) who were the largest taxpayers; (b) how a given individual had reported income and wealth; and (c) what share of VAT was paid by the top 5 percent of taxpayers, and so on. All these operations would have been almost impossible before the arrival of computers.

The next day we met with the Minister of Finance and discussed what assistance we could provide him in the fiscal area. Afterwards, we went to Casablanca and visited the current Director of Customs, Mr. Omari. Mr. Omari was managerial, articulate, informal, and pleasant. We discussed various problems in customs such as smuggling, corruption, and the fall in customs duties that would follow the implementation of the agreement with the European Union, that required Morocco to sharply reduce its import duties. Afterwards he took us to *Le Cabestan*, a restaurant facing the Atlantic and specializing in fish and *fruit de mer*. It was run by Madame Viot, an elderly, French lady who seemed to follow everything that went on in the restaurant with an eagle's eye. I thought that she could have been at home in the movie *Casablanca*. We were told that she was a kind of local institution. The view of the Atlantic and of some rocks on which waves splashed was superb and the food was great. I had *crevettes royales*, or royal shrimps. The shrimps were enormous and were grilled to perfection. Mr. Omari was good company.

In the afternoon we had an appointment with "*Le Patronat*," that is with representatives of the private sector, a kind of Moroccan chamber of commerce. On the way to the appointment we stopped at the Grande Mosque Hasan II, an immense structure built by the current King. It must have been enormously expensive to build. It has a huge tower and a large mosque around it with a plaza in front. It is an impressive building with lots of mosaics. Unfortunately, we were unable to see the interior of the mosque which, we were told, is very beautiful. The setting reminded me of the famous Trani Cathedral in Puglia, Italy, although the mosque is a much larger structure. In both places the building seems to emerge from the sea.

At "*Le Patronat*," a large group of prominent Moroccan entrepreneurs met with us. They were a very articulate, sophisticated, and impressive bunch and the meeting made a big impact on me. They complained strongly about inefficiency in the government and the costs that, not-always-necessary government regulations and procedures imposed on the private sector. The compliance costs of required government authorizations for many private activities were very high, and they needed authorizations for many actions. For some, authorizations bribes needed to be paid. They made the interesting observation that the real cost of a public employee to the economy was much greater than the salary that the employee got because of the economic costs that he/she imposed on society. Thus there is a social cost and a money (salary) cost, and the first may be much larger than the second. Of course this is not always the case. One would hope than in many cases the value of what a public employee contributes to society exceeds the salary that he or she gets.

A public administration can be divided into a productive and an unproductive part. The objective of reforms should be to better compensate the productive part and to eliminate, or at least reduce, the unproductive. The famous Italian economist of the early part of the 20th century, Vilfredo Pareto, understood this problem well. He used to say that in public administrations often 20 percent of the employees do 80 percent of the productive or useful work. It would be nice if one could reduce the unproductive 80 percent so that the productive 20 percent could be better paid and could become even more efficient.

The representatives of the "*Patronat*" argued that the role of the state should be changed to make it a facilitator of private economic activity and not a break on it. This related to a video that the World Customs Organization was preparing at that time in which I had been asked to make a 50 seconds statement arguing that Customs Administrations should *facilitate trade and not impede it.* However, for the 50 second video a TV crew of four had come to Paris, where I was because of an OECD meeting, from London and had spent almost two hours with me. In the video I simply made the observation that governments should only forbid and not authorize. The role of the government should be similar to traffic laws. In market economies private agents should have the right to do all that was explicitly not prohibited without any need to ask for authorization, a need that gave some public employees the power to elicit bribes, often by slowing down the granting of authorizations.

The next day we were invited by the Minister to a luncheon at the Tour Hasan Hotel. A group of World Bank staff had also been invited to the lunch. Kemal Dervis, a capable Turk and then a vice-president at the World Bank, was the senior person in the World Bank group. He would later become Minister of Finance of Turkey and, in 2005, the head of the United Nations Development Program (UNDP). He had come to Rabat to sign a $100 million loan from the World Bank to Morocco and to take part in a large and somewhat unstructured seminar on the implications of globalization for Morocco. There were about ten people in the World Bank group, several with relatively senior ranks. I was often surprised at the Bank's uncoordinated activities and at the number of Bank travelers without clear objectives (at least that is how it seemed to me) for their travels. I always felt that the IMF was a more tightly run institution. I was told that Mr. James Wolfensohn, then the Bank's president, had promised to modernize the whole Moroccan administration when he had met the King. I was curious to see how this would be done.

The luncheon started with *pastilla,* a kind of baked pie with meat and a thin crust. The main dish was a roasted lamb which was brought whole, including the head, to the table and from which the lunch's participants, who beside the World Bank group, included several high-level Moroccan officials, besides the Minister, helped themselves directly. It was followed by a beautiful basket of fruit. The quality of the fruit was exceptional and much better than what one generally got in Washington.

The discussion around the table was about the rising fiscal deficit. The Minister argued that he could not cut public spending because of the high components of expenditure for debt servicing and for salaries. He also reported that I had told him that there had been much progress in the public finances and especially in the tax system of Morocco, that was partly true. I did not want to correct the Minister directly during a social occasion, but I made the observation that if someone is drowning, where the water is 50 feet deep, and he manages to swim to where the water is 20 feet, he has made much progress but he may still drown. The point was that the progress made by Morocco, while significant, might not have been enough.

After lunch we went back to the hotel and discussed what we had learned during the three-day visit. We needed to think of the best strategy to be pursued in our technical assistance to Morocco. I also needed to think about what to report to the Managing Director of the Fund when I returned to give my "back to office report." In the late afternoon we went to the Medina, or the city center, to take a look at the shops. I was again particularly interested in old keys and old locks for my collection. In one shop I saw an interesting Berber lock. The asking price was 450 Dirham which at the time was a significant amount. I was willing to pay 400 Dirham, but the owner of the store flatly refused adding that his son, who had mentioned the price of 450 Dirham, had made a mistake and the price was higher. I tried to bargain to no avail. He did not budge and, on principle, I refused to pay the 450 Dirham. Next door I bought a couple of less interesting locks. Here the man was much nicer and somewhat flexible. At times I felt that a smiling face made it possible for a merchant to get a higher price for an item. Price theory has ignored this aspect unless it is considered an aspect of monopolistic competition. When there is competition, it has assumed that only price determines demand. Later I regretted that because of a silly principle I had missed the opportunity to add a rare Berber lock to my collection. I could not understand why I am generally willing to pay the asking price in a world of fixed prices but never in a world in which bargaining is supposed to be the norm. There must be some deep economic meaning in this attitude. I will leave that to the economic theorists or to psychologists to explain. One of the two locks I bought had a bell that rang when the key was turned. I wondered what function the bell served: to inform those who were inside the house or to scare away potential thieves? Perhaps both, which would show that an instrument can aim to achieve two different objectives, contrary to Tinbergen's theory. Tinbergen a Nobel Prize winner in economics had argued that a policy instrument should only be aimed at a single policy goal.

In the evening, Mr. Ben Brick invited us to dinner at *Les Martinets*, a lovely restaurant with a garden terrace. Once again we had a very good fish dinner following the advice of the old man who was the owner of the restaurant. He obviously wanted to be nice to the Director of Taxation and advised us on what to eat and what not to eat. At the end of the dinner Ben Brick thanked me warmly for past and future assistance to Morocco and presented me with a box containing four old keys. The keys were of average quality, but the gesture was very nice. I insisted on paying for them but he did not want to hear of it. My key collection kept growing. I estimated that the value of the four keys was less than the $100 limits imposed by the Fund on accepting gifts.

I returned to Washington on Royal Air Maroc, which had a direct, convenient flight from Casablanca to New York. The plane, a 747, was practically empty. Royal Air Maroc had been losing a lot of money, especially on the Casablanca–New York flight. What did Morocco get for the lost money? Why do so many countries insist on having national airlines that almost always lose a lot of money?

A final observation: In my travel throughout Morocco I was impressed by the beauty of the country and by its culture. At least at the time of my travels, there seemed to be no animosity against "infidels" and everyone was very friendly. In the Moroccan tax administration a couple of mid-level employees had Jewish backgrounds. It is sad what has happened in recent years, when the prospect of wars of religion has become a distinct possibility and, for a while, the United States had been pursuing a "war on terror." It is ironic that in the age of globalization we may become more and more reluctant to travel to many areas because of terrorism. Hopefully, globalization in the future will not be confined to globalization of goods, excluding globalization of people.

CPSIA information can be obtained at www.ICGtesting.com
Printed in the USA
240527LV00004B/96/P

9 781934 978368